To Peggy
& Mike,

from author and
evangelist,

Dea Warford

EVANGELIST

MY LIFE STORY
MY LIFE JOURNEY

EVANGELIST
DEA WARFORD

Pen &
POWER
Publishing

Edited by Kathie Scriven and Dawn Williams
Cover and formatting by ROOTED Publishing
www.rootedpublishing.com

Published by Pen & Power Publishing

Printed in the United States of America

ISBN: 978-1-7352994-0-2

ACKNOWLEDGMENTS

Evangelist was a project to which many contributed. I thank God for the following:

Jesus, the "author and finisher" of this book (Hebrews 12:2). It was at times almost as though He were writing it, and I was but His scribe. In the middle of the night, He would remind me of past events, truths, and Scriptures to add to this book. If there is any glory deserved for it, He alone is worthy.

Silver L. Fisher, one of my disciples from when I pastored. The autobiography of his life so inspired me that it helped me see the need to share my miraculous journey as well. Read one of the most amazing testimonies of a prayer warrior and personal evangelist: "My Favorite Miracles." Order at amazon.com

Kathie Scrivens, whose professional editing contributed so much. I highly recommend her: kathiescriven@yahoo.com

Dawn Williams, a personal friend and supporter whose experience as an English teacher helped me immensely. We worked closely together in editing to make the book publishable. She contributed as much as anyone to complete this work.

Dana Chatham whose wisdom helped me get started on this book in the beginning and Linda Stephens who did the final editing.

MaryAnn Cazzell, for her help with the Greek language, Karen Ruhl, who updated our website, Barbara De Simon, who helped design our beautiful book cover and formatted the book. She was a real gift from God to me. I can also recommend her: rootedpublishingservices@gmail.com

Pastors Aileen and David Ramirez, my pastors, whose support and love for me is unequaled in any pastor I've served under.

Pastor Terry Risser, who has helped shepherd my family for over a decade. An outstanding story-teller, he authored several books which I recommend you purchase from amazon.com

Angel Garcia and Jennifer Millar, publishing logo designers

Rev. Bob Gaston, a personal friend, and confidant, whose wisdom, prayers, support, and encouragement aided this writing

Warford Ministries Financial supporters, whose love and generosity made it possible for me to spend many hours working on this book. They are truly the fulfillment of the Scripture, "They are a gift to you given by the Lord to do the work" (Numbers 18:6).

Intercessors, and I have many, who helped bear the burden of this ministry on their knees for years and especially during this very difficult project, the writing of my autobiography.

Jody Michels and Sheila Gapinske, mighty prayer warriors, who held my efforts up before the throne of God day and night. I know their prayers helped guide me each day.

My wife, Kathy, who, working quietly in the background, helped sustain this ministry for these five decades and helped bear many burdens along this journey we've made together.

My daughter and her husband, Carissa and Andy Hawksworth, and my son, Nathan, who are all more educated and better writers than I. Their wisdom, training, and experience working with youth as professors at Christian universities helped me know how to better reach the book's target audience, a freshman in college. Are you a freshman? Please read it!

A number of family members and friends who read rough drafts and gave additional advice to me whom I will not take time to mention here, but they know who they are!

And finally, I especially thank God for Pastor Jack Hayford, who without a close second, was the greatest influencer of my life. The class he taught in Personal Evangelism when I was a 17-year-old freshman at LIFE Bible College in Los Angeles transformed my life and ministry forever. Without the foundation Pastor Jack helped establish, these stories would not have been written. My journey shared with you herein would never have occurred. I thank God for Pastor Jack, faithful to his call. I pray for him daily. He is truly a father in the faith to me!

TABLE OF CONTENTS

PREFACE

Pictured on the front cover is Dea Warford and his wife, Kathy taken while they were dating and had just begun their half-a-century journey together.

"Paul's company…entered into the house of Philip the evangelist" (Acts 21:8 KJV).

You are invited to enter the house of Dea the evangelist. Sit down, make yourself at home, and read a candid, personal story that will inspire and help you to add greater eternal significance to your own personal story. Glean transforming truths and grow spiritually from the trials, triumphs, and treasures woven into these true accounts and life lessons.

INTRODUCTION

Paul the Apostle wrote, "I am an apostle...I magnify my ministry" (Romans 11:13). I am an evangelist and I too "magnify my ministry." That is why the title EVANGELIST is in large bold print on the front cover. With this book, I place a magnifying glass into your hands. As you read story after story, you'll see clearly what the unique office of the evangelist is actually about. The word Evangelist comes from the English transliteration for the Greek New Testament word "euvayyelistos," which simply means "a bearer of good news."

Yes, I am a bearer of good news. This book is my autobiography. However, actually, this book tells more about the ministry than the man. The many adventures I relate in this book happened only because God called me and equipped me to be an evangelist. My hope is to inspire you, motivate you, and give helpful examples for how you can witness more effectively for Christ.

Paul exhorted, "Do the work of an evangelist"(2 Timothy 4:5). God wouldn't ask you to do something you couldn't do! Thus, I dared write on the front cover, "You too can DO THE WORK OF AN EVANGELIST." After reading this book, you'll not only know how, but I predict that you will truly desire to be a personal evangelist, and you'll be prepared for future soul-winning opportunities that God will surely delight to bring your way.

I share in this book my fascinating journey...

- I'll tell how I was supernaturally saved from drowning as a child.

- You'll marvel at the thrilling account of how God saved me from a career in the Ku Klux Klan, a white-supremacist organization.

- You'll sit with me in a college classroom, where Pastor Jack Hayford's teaching helped birth this ministry!

- You'll laugh at the funny stories of my many girlfriends, which culminated with meeting and marrying, Kathy, my wife and life-partner.

- I'll share the joys and exciting experiences of being a soul-winner.

Yet, you won't just read absorbing stories. You will learn how to reproduce such soul-winning outcomes in your own life!

On the front cover is a picture of me and my wife, Kathy, taken a half-a-century ago when we were dating and taking a walk. We continue that journey together today. I now invite you to step back with us in time as I recount many milestones in our lives. As I share each adventure, I'll also provide brief teaching with supporting Scriptures on how these experiences can not only inspire you but equip you to do what I am doing.

I am convinced that the greatest harvest of souls ever won to Christ is just ahead of us! This time of reaping will be so ripe with low-hanging fruit that there will not be enough full-time Evangelists, pastors, and other ministers to finish the job. Volunteers are needed! Will you volunteer? "Your people shall be volunteers in the day of Your power" (Psalm 110:3).

Christ told us to...

"Pray the Lord of the harvest to send out laborers into His harvest" (Matthew 9:38).

I prayed that prayer many times! I continue praying that prayer today. Now I'm also putting a tool into the hands of some of those laborers that God is about to send into His harvest. This book is that tool. Do you want to be one of those harvesters? If so, I had you in mind when I wrote it! By the end of this book, you will,

"Be ready at all times to answer anyone who asks you to explain the hope you have in you" (1 Peter 3:15 GNT).

Paul wrote, "Do the work of an evangelist." Because I have walked in the office gift of the evangelist for so many years, I clearly understand that "work." Are you doing that work?

Do you even know what it is?

The stories and teachings will illustrate through true-life dramas why God chose to raise up the biblical office of the evangelist and will demonstrate how this anointing operates.

Walk with Evangelists Dea and Kathy Warford through the next 24 chapters. Are you willing to get to "work"? If so...

Let YOUR adventure begin!

1

SAVED FROM DROWNING

"She called his name Moses, saying, 'Because I drew him out of the water" (Exodus 2:10).

I was drowning! I was four years old. I was drowning and nobody knew it! My sister, Elaine, age nine, and several other children played together in a swimming pool next door to our home in Ontario, California. Two women, mothers of some of the other children, sat on the deck watching us.

My first known picture.

I could not swim at the time. As I waded in the shallow end of the pool, I watched an older boy swim gracefully and safely through the surface of the water. I remember thinking to myself, "Hey, I can do that!" I headed towards the deep end of the pool lifting one arm after the other, imitating his actions. I began to sink, and nobody saw me!

At that very moment, my father, Paul, drove away from our home. He was once a preacher but left the church many years previously. Over time, he became an alcoholic. He drifted from one job to another, usually as a farm laborer. He often fell off the wagon and quit his job or got fired. I still remember one Christmas when I received very little because he was out of work for so long.

That day, my mother left us in Dad's care while she worked at the restaurant she owned. When Dad, a long-term wino, left us at the pool, most likely he was on his way to get a bottle of Port Vino. He was driving… I was drowning.

Suddenly, my dad saw water splash across the front windshield. He pulled over to wipe it off; however, when he got out, no water was on the glass. He looked around and noticed no rain clouds and no sprinklers in the nearby fields. Mystified, Dad started driving again, when suddenly, "swish." Water once again filled the windshield. Though still far from God, my dad's spirit quickly discerned this dramatic sign.

"It's Dea. He's drowning!" Quickly turning the car around, dad raced to the swimming pool, ran up to the two women, and cried, "Where's Dea?" They had lost track of me and had no idea.

My sister was floating in an old inner tube. Dad shouted to her, "Where did you last see Dea?" She pointed in the general vicinity. Dad peered into the water and saw nothing, but he did notice some bubbles rising to the surface.

Dad jumped into the pool without taking off clothing or even his shoes and felt something with his arm. It was me! He pulled me upward toward the surface and laid me face-up on the deck. I coughed and spat and gasped for air. I survived by mere seconds from entering eternity, saved from drowning by a supernatural warning!

Having been a preacher, my dad was familiar with the ways of God. As he looked down, at my 4-year-old frame, both relieved and sobered, he thought to himself, "How many people have lost their children to drowning? Why would God spare Dea?" He knew why: God had a call on my life.

Yes, God indeed had a call on my life, though it would take many years and many experiences for me to discover God's purpose for that call. I know now that my call was to be preacher of the gospel. I am a full-time bearer of good news and have been for many years. Evangelist: that is both my career and my calling.

What are you called to do?

You likely have a different career and a different calling. However, God nevertheless still calls you, at least in some measure, to "Do the work of an evangelist" (2 Timothy 4:5). Saving the lost is an evangelist's most important work, thus God has given me the assignment to write this book in order to help you to not only understand how but as the Word says, to "do" it!

At my third birthday party.

God told a prophet to "Write the vision and make it plain… That he may run who reads it" (Habakkuk 2:2). I will endeavor to make this "vision" easy to understand and interesting to read. Once it is "plain" and clearly understood, my hope is that you will then begin to "run" with conviction and joy to…

"Do the work of an evangelist."

Like me, you may be called to be a full-time evangelist. May the milestones of my life inspire and perhaps better clarify what God wants to do through you. You may be holding down a secular job yet sense a call to walk in the evangelist's office. You don't have to quit your job or career to evangelize. Many pastors today work secular jobs while pastoring a church. Everyone, yes, that means you reader, is called, as the opportunity arises, as the Spirit leads; at work, at school, among friends, with relatives and neighbors, to be, for at least a moment in time, an evangelist!

You likely can relate to my story of how God saved me from death as a child. Were you saved from death at some point in your life: in a car accident, from a disease, by an invisible angel assigned to keep you alive? Could it be that God reserved you and "brought you to the kingdom for such a time as this?" (Esther 4:14).

The name Moses means "drawn out of the water." Moses was supernaturally saved out of water because he was destined to be the deliverer of millions of Israelites in bondage. I too was supernaturally saved out of water. I know it was because I was given the destiny to save many people who are drowning in sin and sinking down into hell.

If by being a bearer of good news in the final harvest you save just one soul from hell, to that one soul you will be throughout eternity the most important person who ever came into their life!

As we explore what are likely uncharted territories for you, walk beside me on "the sawdust trail" as the traveling life of an evangelist is often described. I discovered many treasures along this trail. Please allow me to open a personal treasure chest and share some of my most cherished memories.

Read my adventures and may they serve as a catalyst to help you also to . . .

Unearth more fabulous treasures along your life pathway.

An Evangelist fulfilling his destiny by calling people to the altar to repent and get right with God.

Dea's uncle, Connie Lynch, preaching at a Ku Klux Klan rally in St. Augustine, Florida, 1964 (Used by permission from The Saturday Evening Post, 8/22/1964 issue).

2

KU KLUX KLAN DECEPTION

"Then many false prophets will rise up and deceive many" (Matthew 24:11).

My uncle, Charles (Connie) Lynch, wearing a vest made of a Civil War Confederate flag, preached powerfully from behind the podium at the Ambassador Auditorium in Los Angeles in 1965. He enthralled the audience of like-minded segregationists whose goal was to preserve the white race from the perceived corruption and inferiority of Jewish and black people. The Ku Klux Klan stood as very dedicated opponents of the Civil Rights Movement of the 1960s. As a young teenager, I watched and listened intently, enthralled with the excitement of such a historic moment, and proud to see my own uncle leading the rally.

My dad, one of several in the auditorium wearing Brown Shirt uniforms similar to those worn by the Sturmabteilung, the German Nazi Party's original paramilitary wing, sat beside me. I clearly remember my uncle helping my dad get into the outfit. Dad wanted to show his loyalty to the cause and support his brother-in-law, but I discerned Dad's reluctance to wear a Nazi-type uniform. While my uncle spoke, some of the men in uniform interrupted the proceedings, rising to their feet to shout, "JEWS!"

Uncle Connie had not always been a racist. At one time, he was a preacher of the Gospel. My parents said he could fill the altars with seekers prayerfully responding to his powerful messages. But, later, Connie left the church for unknown reasons and was no longer in ministry.

One day, a stranger knocked at the door of Connie's house. After being invited inside, the man sat with Connie awhile and proceeded to persuade him of the doctrine of the superiority of the white race. He probably was also the one who convinced him that the Jews were the enemy. Feeling he had done his job, the man walked out the door. Connie looked out the window to watch him as he left, but he was nowhere to be seen!

Was it an angel of darkness that deceived Connie? I am convinced that the answer is yes. Tragically, Connie converted into a preacher spreading the message of white supremacy.

By the time I was in junior high school, a distortion of religion which we in the 21st century simply refer to as racism became a way of life for our family. In the 1960s, my uncle joined the Ku Klux Klan and eventually became reputed as the "best preacher in the Ku Klux Klan." The U.S. House Subcommittee on Un-American Activities, during that period, claimed Connie Lynch was, "the most dangerous man in America."

The governor of the state of Mississippi once even offered Connie $20,000 if he would leave the state and never come back. In today's dollars, that would be worth about $160,000. Connie rejected the offer because he genuinely believed in the message he preached.

My uncle was an intelligent, witty, fiery communicator. I was in awe of him. During the height of the Civil Rights Movement, Connie spoke at Klan rallies throughout the southern states. The media and government considered him responsible for inciting white riots in Bogalusa, Louisiana, and St. Augustine, Florida. He spent over a year in jail for inciting a riot in Baltimore!

Often, Connie returned to Ontario, California where I lived, and he sometimes stayed with us while in the area. I remember him putting his big loaded pistol up on the bed board at night, close at hand in case he needed it. As I grew a little older, I became his protégé. He began to teach me the "truths" of the KKK. He used the Bible to support many of his theories concerning the superiority of the white race. He taught me that the white race which spread throughout Europe and America was in reality the descendants of the 10 lost tribes of Israel. Connie believed these tribes, other than Judah and Benjamin, were carried away captive by the Assyrians and later spread throughout Europe. Connie taught that the "true Israel of God," the white race, was really "God's chosen people" and not the present-day Jews!

Since the Bible says in Romans 11:26, "All Israel shall be saved," Connie taught that every white person on earth, no matter how much they may have sinned, would ultimately be saved and go to heaven. As a teenager, indoctrinated into this kind of teaching, I lived a very sinful life. My attitude and viewpoint became - Why live a holy life if you are going to go to heaven anyway?

According to Connie and the KKK platform, present-day Jews were not really Israelites. Their line of reasoning taught that the Jews were a race, part-human, part-satanic: the result of sexual intercourse between Satan and Eve, the real forbidden fruit. Since Jews were children of the devil, they were really the synagogue of Satan. Connie used two Scriptures to teach support for claiming this unholy union. Revelation 2:9 states, "I know the blasphemy of those who say they are Jews and are not, but are a synagogue of Satan." Connie also tied his analysis to Revelation 3:9, "I will make those of the synagogue of Satan, who say they are Jews and are not, but lie -- indeed I will make them come and worship before your feet, and to know that I have loved you."

Based on this line of thinking, Connie believed that we should kill all Jews. He used Luke 19:27, taken out of context, to justify his view, "But bring here those enemies of mine, who did not want me to reign over them, and slay them before me." I did not especially like the idea of killing people, but I believed that my uncle surely knew best! Connie further taught that the Bible was written as a book "only for the white race." Jesus came only to save His own people of Israel, the Anglo/Saxons. Connie vehemently believed that blacks could not be included. Blacks were, in fact, probably aliens from another planet brought here on spaceships, and so they should be shipped back to Africa where they had come from.

Connie Lynch

The core of my family changed under Connie's influence. My sister, Elaine, started out as a godly Christian and church attendee. Connie also deceived her. Elaine left the church in her late teen years and began dancing in local bars. My dad believed and spoke a line of reasoning much like Connie's. Over time, friends and other family members were greatly influenced by my persuasive uncle who knew how to use Bible verses to twist the message to support his assertions.

As Connie began to teach me how to argue our racist ideology, I took hate literature to my high school and debated with classmates. I brought National States Rights Party newspapers called the *Thunderbolt* to school. I didn't realize it then, as I was passionate about the mission, but these newspapers were a cheap, hateful, trashy tool to fan the flames of racial hatred. I still remember parts of an anti-Jewish poem I read in the *Thunderbolt*. A fictional Jewish man was apparently describing his heinous plans and purpose on earth. I only remember one stanza, but it went something like this:

> "My greasy women are sloppy and fat,
> but them I choose to bear my brats,
> I am a filthy hook-nosed Jew."

The hate-filled spirit that possessed Hitler was apparently alive and well. That same spirit was also deceiving me.

Connie's influence in my life and the literature I was reading and promoting occurred during the height of the 1960s civil-rights debates in America. We discussed the issues often and passionately in our high school classes. I engaged in debates at school about white superiority. However, whenever I couldn't defend my viewpoint against student's or teacher's arguments, I went home to my uncle and told him what we discussed. Having finely honed his debate skills through years of racist thinking and preaching, Connie always gave me the appropriate response which I eagerly took back to my school.

For example, one time, a teacher met me in the hallway and asked me, "Are you, Dea Warford?" I affirmed that I was. He then pulled a pencil out of his pocket, held it to my attention, and said, "Your mind is as narrow as this pencil." I had no answer. Embarrassed and frustrated, I went home and reported to Connie. He told me to tell that teacher, "Jesus said it is a straight and narrow way that leads to truth." He was a skilled debater and had an answer to everything. I worshiped my uncle, almost to my ruin.

We began to attend a little church called, "The Church of Jesus Christ Christian," where Connie often preached. Many in this odd church of racists believed Jesus' name was really Seliah, which they claim was revealed to them through a prophetic word. So, they would sing hymns using the name Seliah instead of Jesus. Surely, Satan laughed as they unwittingly praised him instead of the one true Lord of the universe.

The members of this little church promoted another peculiar belief. They believed white people, as God's chosen race, could live on earth without ever having to experience death. Seliah? Never die? Once people accept a false premise as the foundation for their theology, it gives place to all kinds of other falsehoods. One lie always leads to more lies. The "Father of lies" (John 8:44) was drowning my family and me in a deep pool of deception.

Some people in that strange church believed Christ would return to earth to lead the white race in a final battle against Jews and blacks. Concerning this epic final battle, Connie Lynch was quoted in the nationally published *Saturday Evening Post* magazine, which I proudly brought to high school to show off to my friends:

"'There's gonna be a bloody race riot all over this nation," he said. 'The stage is being set for the earth to get a bloodbath.'

And then his mouth hardened. His cold, dark eyes looked straight ahead.

'When the smoke clears,' he said,

'there ain't gonna be nothin' left except white faces.'"

Connie's teachings became a solemn business to me. Race, in fact, became the most crucial thing in the universe. I actually believed that I had a call of God to preach a gospel of white superiority. Under a dark cloud of deception, my goal in life became to help preserve the white race, to ship blacks back to Africa, and, if necessary, kill Jews. My highest goal, at one time, was to become the Imperial Wizard of the Ku Klux Klan, and champion its message with power and grandeur like my uncle.

The die had been cast for my life, or so I thought. But God had a much different idea and life path for me! Why? Because God called me to be an evangelist, not a rabble-rousing racist!

Even as I retell this true story, my past seems like fiction. But, it all happened. I know. I lived it. The KKK teachings may sound absurd and one might imagine, "How could someone possibly actually believe such things?" That's easy to answer, but tragic, nevertheless. Because of the amazing power of deception, *those who are deceived don't realize they are deceived*. Tragically, Connie was deluded, and he, in turn, deceived me and many others.

Connie's sense of truth was twisted, and Connie's gospel of white supremacy was not good news. Jesus warned concerning the Last Days...

"Take heed that no one deceives you" (Matthew 24:2).

Why?

"For false Christs and false prophets will rise and show great signs and wonders to deceive, if possible, even the elect" (Matthew 24:24).

We, Christians, are the elect and we must not be deceived! Rather, we should be prepared to help rescue the deceived out of their deception.

Thank God, after walking years through the dark valley of racism, I discovered that Jesus was waiting to take my hand and lead me out of the KKK and back in the right direction.

"You will show me the path of life" (Psalm 16:11).

The Lord was about to "show me the path of life."

I had a call on my life to be an evangelist and to evangelize others, but first. . .

Somebody had to *evangelize* me!

3

SAVED OUT OF THE
KU KLUX KLAN

**"And you will seek Me and find Me, when you search
for Me with all your heart" (Jeremiah 29:13).**

Uncle Connie hoodwinked most of my immediate family through his
teachings. However, I had another uncle, Marvin Williams, who also was

a preacher. Unlike some of us,
Marvin was NOT duped by the Ku
Klux Klan's lies and deceptions. He
loved the Bible more than anybody I
have ever met. All he wanted to talk
about were the Scriptures.

Because Marvin so passionately
studied the Bible for many years, he
readily knew scriptural quotes. One
day, as I discussed some of my beliefs
with Marvin, he quoted II Thess.

**My dad, Paul, and Uncle
Marvin +/-1945.**

2:11-12 and said, "Dea, the Bible says you can believe a lie and be damned." Those words wrenched my heart! As I mulled over what he said, I thought to myself, You can believe a lie and be damned for it? What if I am believing a lie? What if I am going to end up in hell for it?" That reality check scared me, but also motivated me.

"The fear of the Lord is the beginning of wisdom" (Prov. 9:10).

Marvin's spoken truth from the Word of God birthed in me a resolute pursuit of wisdom motivated by the instinctive desire to escape an eternity in hell. Marvin did "the work of an evangelist" in seeking to help me know the truth. I decided to follow Christ without even realizing it at the time. Christ is "The Way, the Truth, and the Life" (John 14:6). I wanted to follow the truth wherever it took me; however, it was not an immediate gotcha moment. As a result of Marvin's warning, my first rhema, a personal word from God, I began studying the Bible on my own during the last semester of my junior year in high school. Jesus said, "Search the Scriptures, for in them you think you have eternal life, and they are they which testify of me" (John 5:39).

I began searching the Scriptures!

Previously, I always let my Uncle Connie tell me what the Bible taught and meant. I never researched the Word of God on my own. Therefore, I determined that I would read the New Testament with an open mind and heart, with one goal: to discover the truth about racism.

I lived like any other teenage sinner during the day, but every night, before I went to bed, I knelt at my bedside and prayed this sincere prayer, "God, reveal to me the truth!" Then, I read a few chapters in the New Testament: Matthew, Mark, Luke, and so on.

I decided to no longer take for granted that my church was right, as so many Americans do. My father's religion was not good enough for me, especially if following that path would result in my eternal punishment in hell! The necessary transformation did not happen overnight. However, as I studied the Word, slowly but surely, light began to dawn on my soul.

I progressively realized that Jesus did not teach segregation, but rather salvation. He did not teach hatred, but instead love. The truth became clear. I felt conviction, so I visited a church and talked with the pastor concerning this struggle of faith. He led me in the sinner's prayer. I tried to do right and be a Christian, I really did! But whenever I hung around Uncle Connie again, with his persuasive ways, I basically reverted to his racist ideas.

About this time also, my school life began to unravel. I became quite verbal about white supremist beliefs: taking literature to school, having my uncle speak at an off-campus high school club, arguing my views vehemently in classes. With such activities, it was not long before parents got wind of my racist stance on campus. Several parents called the school office to complain.

One day, the vice-principal and my counselor brought me into their office to learn more about my beliefs. As they asked questions and tape recorded my replies, I openly shared with them what I believed. Things moved quickly. I was getting nervous! The clashes in our nation and our local community over racism escalated during the 1960's. At

My high school graduation picture.

the time, I stood strong and passionately promoted the racist cause. Soon after the meeting with the school administrators, a dream and other evolving events gave me reason to fear for my safety or even my life. God has a sense of humor: I dreamed that some African natives were boiling me in a big pot! God was circumstantially showing me that the path I was following was indeed a lie and would end in tragedy for me.

Concerned about the difficulties and hostilities I faced at school because of my racist beliefs, I decided to graduate a year early from high school. To do this, I took a summer class at high school and a few extra units at a local community college. Believe it or not, this was my actual reasoning at the time: I figured God wanted me to graduate from high school a year early so that I could send the blacks back to Africa a year earlier.

At age 17, I registered at California State Polytechnic College (Cal Poly) to begin classes in the fall of 1966 planning to major in social science. I figured that if I expected people to believe me when I announced that Caucasians were intellectually superior to other races, it would help if I had letters behind my name. To complete my necessary units to graduate from high school early, I enrolled in a summer history class at the high school and a speech class at a nearby junior college.

In that college speech class, the teacher assigned a debate on segregation versus integration. Of course, you know what stance I took. In the debates, I reverted to defending white supremacy as I had so many times before. Later in the summer, my turn finally came to give my speech. With a last name that begins with "W," since grammar school, I was usually one of the last people called upon in class.

Since I had been reading the New Testament each night in my pursuit of truth, though clearly not yet delivered from my racist leanings, I now was more inclined to talk about Christ's teaching on salvation, though I certainly did not fully understand what that meant at the time!

Therefore, when I rose to deliver my speech in class, I announced my speech's title as "The Wisdom of Christ." My very first sermon! Quoting from the gospels, I spoke of how Jesus wisely dealt with all antagonists. I explained that my "controlling purpose" for my speech was to "lead you on the road to salvation." What a contradistinctive thing to preach after arguing vehemently for racial separation!

After each student gave his or her speech, the custom was for the other students to anonymously critique the speech on paper and give their comments to the speaker. As I perused the comments, one person wrote, "You lost me!" Another, "You sound like a revivalist." How interesting! That is exactly what I became!

However, it was another person's comment which cut to my heart. Obviously a Christian, he or she wrote, "How do you think your stand for civil rights affects your testimony for Christ?"

Those words of truth brought a flood of revelation and conviction. Clearly, I must choose one of two courses: be a preacher for the Ku Klux Klan or be a preacher of the gospel of Christ. I could not be both.

I was in the throes of my life's most pivotal decision! However, I still lived in sin and was not saved!

I discover the real Connie Lynch.

About that time, my Uncle Connie came over to our house again. This time he was drunk. I knew that he had been sleeping with a woman. He was divorced from my aunt at the time. This disturbed me deeply. That evening, while I was playing the piano in the living room, Connie drunkenly walked over to the bench, put one foot on it and boasted, "Play Connie Lynch! Play Connie Lynch!"

I discerned pride in him which I had never seen before. I was deeply disappointed. Here I was, getting ready to throw all caution to the wind, to give up any chance of a meaningful career, possibly endangering my life, dedicated to the cause that my uncle championed. Yet, there he stood with his foot on the piano bench, drunk, sleeping around, proudly wanting us to celebrate in song the accomplishments of the great Connie Lynch.

Connie belied with his words and actions, what he'd convinced me of through the years: that this fight for the white race was worth any sacrifice. My deep respect for him shattered, and my doubts about racism further deepened. My path out of error was at hand!

Just weeks before beginning college classes at Cal Poly to help forward my career in the Klan, I attended Camp Cedar Crest, Foursquare Church youth camp in the San Bernardino Mountains of Southern California. During this camp, the accumulation of months of self-doubt and self-examination in my pursuit of truth headed rapidly towards a climactic conclusion.

After a guest speaker preached in a chapel service, he gave an invitation to come to the front as a sign of surrender to Christ, also known as an altar call. I answered that call and joined others in prayer around the altar area, at last ready to completely renounce racism and embrace true salvation. My life took a beautiful 180-degree turn for the better!

In the mid-1960s, I certainly had no idea that as an evangelist I would one day, like that guest speaker, be preaching the gospel and giving thousands of altar calls! In fact, about a decade or so later, I was the nightly guest speaker preaching in that very chapel and giving altar calls!

While still at camp, a few days after my decision for Christ, I awakened at 4 AM to a deep sense in my soul that God was calling me to preach. I knelt at my bunk bed in our cabin and committed myself to God's purpose.

After camp, I announced to my mother that instead of going to Cal Poly, I was going to a little Bible College that was unaccredited at that time. My mother emphatically said, "You're not going!" She had other career plans for her son! But, God had plans too.

During those last few weeks of summer, my father and I worked together on a farm in Chino inoculating ducks. I told him of God's call on my life, and my desire to prepare for the ministry in Bible College. Remember, my dad was once a preacher. He had unfortunately chosen alcohol over the ministry. His chance had apparently passed him by. However, that didn't mean his son should miss out on his opportunity.

Perhaps God reminded him of that day at the swimming pool thirteen years earlier when he saved me from death and God brought my call to my dad's attention. Mindful of that call, my dad then announced, "Son, you can go to Bible College. I'll have a talk with your mom."

Over my mom's remonstrations, she and I drove to the Cal Poly's registrar's office. They returned the social science studies enrollment deposit, and right afterwards we drove to enroll me in LIFE Bible College.

August of 1966, I became a new creature in Christ (2 Corinthians 5:17). Connie's influence on my life was gone at last! Before long, the Church of Jesus Christ Christian closed down. My uncle Connie died of heart disease at 59 years of age in 1972. Sadly. to our knowledge, he never renounced the lies he preached!

Thank God, however, my father renounced his racism and entered the ministry again, pastoring fifteen years before his retirement. He is now in heaven! Other family members followed me in revoking our racist past and returning to Christ.

My sister graduated from LIFE Bible College and became a teacher of the Word. She has flown with me many times to prophesy, with a prophet's mantle, and teach alongside her evangelist brother.

What a joyful irony: I have preached the message of God's love in not only white, but also black, Hispanic, Asian, and multicultural churches around America. I have also held International crusades in other than predominantly white nations like Mexico, Costa Rica, and India!

An African American who accepted Christ.

As I preach in churches, I can honestly report that I love the ethnic cultures and races in those services every bit as much as members of my race! I love Jewish people too and would gladly preach in a synagogue if they would let me! Jesus truly is the answer to racism and virtually every other problem people face. I now clearly see the truth that "Man looks on the outward appearance but God looks on the heart" (1 Samuel 16:7).

In retrospect, I genuinely believe that if I had continued in Connie's deception, I would be dead now: dead from an assassin's bullet, dead from a sinful lifestyle, or dead by the judging hand of a holy God. I certainly would be eternally lost! Instead, to God alone be the glory, I am a full-time evangelist.

I stand as living evidence that hope abounds for anyone lost and deceived by any false teaching. Those who have followed my teachings and preaching through the years can perhaps better understand why I take such a strong stand for right doctrinal interpretation of the Bible. A wrong interpretation was leading me and my family towards hell!

Are you believing a lie?

Reader, are you believing a lie that could cause your soul to be damned? If you are not sure, I highly recommend you do what I did. Start reading the Bible with an open heart and mind. Humbly ask the Lord to reveal the truth to you. Trust me: this is a prayer the Lord delights in answering!

Reading the Bible on my own as a 17-year-old saved me from hell! Is God calling you to study the Bible more? "If you continue in my Word... you shall know the truth and the truth shall make you free" (John 8:31, 32).

As we wrap up this chapter, consider for a moment the people in your circle of influence. How many of them are deceived: by a false leader, a false religion, the devil's lies, or ignorance of the truth?

Think about it! A relative of mine boldly shared the Scriptures with me and warned me that I could "believe a lie and be damned." His witness, his evangelizing me with the truth, resulted in not only my salvation, but ultimately in the fulfillment of my call as a full-time evangelist.

Won't you, like my Uncle Marvin, share the Word of God and your testimony with someone today? If you will, you might change their life forever, like mine was changed forever. Will you…

"Do the work of an evangelist" (2 Tim. 4:5).

4

GRAMMAR SCHOOL TO BIBLE COLLEGE

"When I was a child, I spoke and thought and reasoned as a child. But when I grew up, I put away childish things" (1 Corinthians 13:11 NLT).

To better understand my journey, we must first go back and review some of my earlier experiences. Life for kids in America back in the 1950's was different than it is today. My sister and I often slept outside in the front yard on summer nights, and our front yard had no fence! I had free rein to wander far and wide to explore with four friends about my age who also lived in the neighborhood.

While still in grammar school, during the summers, while my mother and dad worked, I stayed at home, often by myself. Daycares did not exist back then. If I got my hands on a dollar bill, I took the bus, by myself, to downtown Ontario, California, 38 miles east of Los Angeles. Back then, I could get something to eat, a cool toy, and bus fare there and back for a buck! I often tried to get my mom a little something as a peace offering, but she always responded, "Money burns a hole in your pocket!"

The summer after second grade, I walked a mile to a church for

Vacation Bible School. Kids were used to walking back then. In that little Church of God, I answered my first altar call and gave my heart to Christ. Something happened too! When I got home, I joyfully told my mother and sister, "I got saved today!" I think it stuck for a while, as sometimes I went to church with my sister, read the Bible a little, and prayed. However, I can't remember doing anything else that Christians should do.

I still remember what I was taught at the Gospel Tabernacle where my sister got saved. This very legalistic church somehow led to my childish conclusion that to be a Christian was simple. According to their rules,

"Christians don't go to movie theaters, dances, gamble, drink or smoke."

I felt that if I could just avoid those temptations, then my salvation was secure. I actually believed that if I attended a movie theater, if Jesus came while I was sitting there, I would miss the rapture.

Life went along fine, until Walt Disney's 1959 film *Shaggy Dog* played at the Granada Theater downtown. Some of my friends planned to go on a Saturday, and I could not resist the temptation to join them. When I first sat down in the theater, I felt so guilty, a deep foreboding. After all, what if Jesus came while I was there? That conviction continued but began to gradually disappear the longer I watched the movie. This moment marked the beginning of my drift away from the Lord.

That backward slide was not, of course, the fact that I was watching a wholesome movie in a darkened room. The change came as the result of a decision repeated throughout history by those drifting from the straight and narrow way. I was willing to walk away from my Lord, if that is what it took, for what I thought was one little taste of sin. Thus, I followed in the vein of Esau, who, "for one morsel of food, sold his birthright" (Hebrews 12:16).

One of the saddest Scriptures in the Bible is in 2 Tim. 4:10 (GW): "Demas has abandoned me. He fell in love with this present world"

John's warning in 1 John 3:15 was a warning I failed to heed: "Do not love the world or the things of the world."

Once I could slip off to a movie, it became easier to sneak a cigarette with my friends, listen to dirty jokes, or even, God forbid, play poker. By the time I was in junior high, I believe I had reverted to an unsaved state, behaving just like my friends around me. The last thing I wanted to be when I grew up was a preacher! But, God wasn't through with me yet! After the 8th grade, a cousin who attended a Foursquare Gospel Church invited me to join him that summer for a week at Camp Cedar Crest by coming along with him and some from his church youth group. I did so.

President of DeAnza Junior High School.

Once again, as in 2nd grade, when the altar call was given, I went forward to recommit my life to Christ. I must also have felt a call at the time because the guest speaker at that Jr. High Camp, Reverend Bob Inglis, many years later told me so. When I was holding a revival at the church where He was pastoring, he reported that at that junior high camp I had said to him, "I feel a call to preach. Should I go now or wait and first go to Bible College?" Recounting the moment, we both laughed.

Unfortunately, when I started high school and returned to running around with my old friends, I forgot what happened at that summer camp. The next summer, my cousin invited me to go back to camp with him, but I turned him down because I had a chance to work at a farm the same week as camp. If I helped the farmer harvest his grapes, I could make enough money to buy a surfboard. I chose the surfboard. This time, it wasn't a movie, but a sport which lured me from Christ.

Two summers later, however, I attended the camp again. For the third time, I walked down the aisle to the altar to surrender to the Lord. Maybe this time, after returning home, it would be a permanent change. But, just a week or two later, I was in a car with my cousin, David Williams, Marvin Williams' son, and an older friend who was driving. I noticed a girl walking on the sidewalk. I said, "Check that out, David!" He retorted, "I thought you got saved at camp!"

I thought I had too, but then if so, why had I lusted after a girl? The devil put it into my heart, and I believed him, "Well, I guess you aren't saved anymore are you?" Again, I gave up and walked away from the Lord. For those who desire to do the work of an evangelist, please see the importance of helping new converts get settled into a local church and helping them understand some of the fundamentals of the faith: like one sin does not an unsaved Christian make! More about helping new converts in chapter 21.

Thus, unfortunately, I spent another year in sin. That was also the year I got heavily involved in the KKK's teachings. I felt a strong call to defend the faith of white supremacy. One Saturday night, after a formal dance at my high school, we parked for a while, in a somewhat remote place.

She asked me what I wanted to be after my education. I told her I wanted to be a preacher in the Ku Klux Klan. She immediately lost all interest in me and soon insisted that I take her home. I suppose that I viewed it as a price we committed Klansmen had to pay for our convictions!

This brings us again to the summer after high school. Full of anticipation during the drive up the mountains to Camp Cedar Crest, I sensed something significant was about to happen. I had previously registered to start classes at Cal Poly to further my racist career, yet I felt a persistent nagging at my heart to preach Christ instead. I had NOT fully decided which one yet.

My mother and David's mother rode in the front seat taking us to camp. David and I sat in the back, talking, laughing and anticipating meeting the girls! To prepare ourselves, we brought along a huge trunk packed with all our cool clothes to enable us to be the chick-magnets we considered ourselves.

However, the Holy Spirit was also at that camp, and I was soon at the altar surrendering to the Lord's call to salvation, saved, yet still struggling with my call to ministry. One morning, one of the leaders announced a special meeting in the prayer room of Chalfant Auditorium for anyone interested in learning more about LIFE Bible College. I decided to check it out. A professor from LIFE told us about the school and answered some of the questions from the small group of teenagers present.

I distinctly remember their little college catalog, thin and cheaply made, especially compared to the big, exciting catalog of the California Polytechnic State College where I was already enrolled. I was not impressed. Besides, at that moment, I was concentrating more on a girl named Mary, the cutest blue-eyed blonde I had met and fallen head-over-heels for at camp that week. We sat together during services and spent time in the afternoons together. At that moment, Bible College did not impress me.

I was usually the earliest riser in my cabin, so I took my shower, got dressed, and then sat on a log outside Mary's cabin waiting to walk with her to the morning services. Her girlfriends noticed me outside and hollered back to her, "Mary, Dea's here!" As I patiently waited, I sang Beatles songs to myself, yet loud enough for others to enjoy my soloist voice, of course.

Then one morning, the Lord surprised me. At about 4 AM, during the middle of the seven-day camp, He woke me up. At that moment, I felt God call me to preach the gospel of Christ, NOT the KKK's gospel. Kneeling at my bunk, I quietly prayed one of the most dedicated, selfless prayers that any evangelist could ever pray. I said, "Lord, as long as you give me Mary as my girlfriend, I'll do my best to become a Foursquare preacher." Wasn't I an instant spiritual giant!?!

Usually, after girls got to know me a little better, they wanted nothing to do with me. Most friendships lasted hours, days, or a few weeks. Thank God! The Lord, in His great wisdom, knew that, unstable as I was, I needed someone in my life at that time to help ground me in that Bible College. That someone was Mary.

LIFE Bible College

I applied to LIFE Bible College. My grades were fine, but the admissions people were apparently troubled about the fact that I was a new convert. I had not proven myself yet nor shown stability as a Christian, much less as a leader in the body of Christ. I went to the Foursquare Church near my house and sat down with a woman on staff. After hearing my testimony and the genuineness of my call to preach, she helped me out by becoming my advocate and personal champion.

I do not know what she told the college authorities, but she convinced them, and they decided to admit me on a probationary basis. Imagine my excitement after dad cleared the path with my mom and this assisting minister cleared it with the administration. Now I could attend LIFE instead of Cal Poly. Only one more hurdle remained. I needed to move into a room in the college dormitories.

I cannot express my thrill as mom drove me to the LIFE Bible College campus directly across the street from the famous Echo Park in Los Angeles. She parked our car in front of the college, an imposing five-story building, and we headed upstairs to the registrar's office.

As we sat in front of the registrar's desk to enroll and reserve a dorm room, we were greeted with the news that there were no more rooms left in the dorms. The man said he was sorry. I was too! My mother and I walked out. I couldn't believe this was happening. God called me here! He helped me every step of the way. This could not be happening!

Then, at the very moment we were getting into the car to drive away forever, I heard a voice cry out, "Dea!" I looked across the street to see David Palmer, one of my cabin counselors at camp. We became friends at camp and sat together for some services. He was a student at LIFE. "What are you doing here?" he asked.

I explained that I came to register for college and get a room in the dorms but was told that no dorm rooms were available. He shot back, "I am a senior! I can have whomever I want as my roommate." Excited, together we marched right back upstairs to the registrar's office. Within an hour, I was officially enrolled in Bible College.

A series of small miracles occurred to get a newly converted, immature teenager into that Christian College. It was truly ideal for my needs. Instead of my unsaved friends, I was surrounded by committed Christians. My roommate, David, was the most spiritually-minded person I had ever met!

David probably was sorry many times that he welcomed me into his abode. More than once he walked into the room and immediately turned off the blaring rock-and-roll songs! Once I peered through our window and noticed a gal walking by outside. I told David the same comment I told my cousin, David, "Check that out!" I wasn't prepared for his response. He didn't say, "I thought you were saved." Instead, he gently said, "Dea, I ask the Lord to help me to see a woman's soul!" I never forgot that. To be a soul-winner, we must seek to see both women's and men's souls!

To mold me as an evangelist, the Lord arranged and rearranged many circumstances in my life. Through His infinite wisdom, the Lord also helps arrange many circumstances in your life. He does this because He loves you and wants you to be happy and successful. But, I am convinced, it is also so that you can do the work of an evangelist.

Consider for a moment: He gave you a job, your neighborhood, your church, your friends, etc. These things were given to you as a part of your destiny. I believe God has a work for you to do as one of His representatives on earth.

Your work will include being a witness for Him...

"First I predicted your rescue, then I saved you and proclaimed it to the world. No foreign god has ever done this. You are witnesses that I am the only God" (Isaiah 43:12 NLT).

Very soon the Lord is going to move mightily on earth and is going to sweep millions of lost people from all over the globe into His kingdom.

You can play a vital part in that short, but glorious season of revival before He returns!

"For He will finish the work and cut it short in righteousness, Because the Lord will make a short work upon the earth." (Romans 9:28)

All of my journey and all of your journey up to this point of our lives could be primarily but preparation for this one future, brief period, one...

Climactic, Crowning, Cosmic Conclusion!

What a thrilling thought! For the time being, though, let me take you back in time again...

As I began to experience Bible College, His plan for my life slowly came into focus. You will learn more about His ways from His dealings with me.

Again I say, God puts people, places, and circumstances in our path to help us fulfill our calling. In the next chapter, you'll see how God did that very thing in my life.

As you continue reading this book, prayerfully ask the Lord...

"Within my present circumstances, how can I best prepare myself to do the work of an evangelist?"

5

MARY, MY FIRST LOVE, AND MY FIRST LOVE FOR SOULS

"I, Jeremiah, said, 'Almighty Lord, I do not know how to speak. I am only a boy! But the Lord said to me, 'Don't say, that you are only a boy. You will go wherever I send you. You will say whatever I command you to say.' Then the Lord stretched out his hand and touched my mouth. The Lord said to me, 'Now I have put my words in your mouth'"
(Jeremiah 1:6, 7, 9 GW).

After moving into the dorms, I settled into a routine that lasted for some time. My college classes all met in the morning, and I worked part-time in the afternoon for UPS for a while, then for a fast food restaurant called Pioneer Chicken.

While hitchhiking on Sunset Boulevard to that chicken restaurant in Hollywood a few miles away from campus, a policeman stopped where I stood at the curb and issued me a ticket. I learned that in L.A. when hitchhiking, I must keep at least one foot on the sidewalk. I had no idea that was a law!

Suitcase full of clean clothes my mom had washed and off to Bible College as a freshman.

My mother realized that for me to work, I needed a car. So, she gave me her modern 1965 VW Bug. I still remember the moment, after coming home for the weekend, I proudly drove off our property with MY car to head back to the college. See the picture of me heading back to the dorms on the left. My Mom took the bus to work until she found another car for herself. A mother's love: the greatest love in the universe! That VW, the most overrated vehicle in history, was my very first car which I drove all four years while in college. With a car, I not only drove to work, but I also drove to Mary's house, often!

I was so in love with Mary! Many mornings, I lingered in bed before classes and daydreamed about her, often reliving that precious week at summer camp. Before I got my car, we talked on the phone, wrote to each other, and I sometimes hitched a ride with friends who lived in her area so I could see her.

Within a few weeks after meeting, she broke the news to me over the phone that she decided she was going to start dating Rick again, her unsaved boyfriend she dated before she came to camp and rededicated her life to Christ. She explained, "I want to try to lead him to Christ." Devastated, I hung up the phone. My first true love was now dating another man, I mean, another boy!

I immediately started on a water-only fast hoping God would restore

Mary to me. I often went to the prayer room in the Angeles Auditorium at the college and cried out to God. Over and over, I lamented, "Lord, I'm willing to give up Mary, if it's Your will, but PLEASE DON'T TAKE HER AWAY!" A few hours later, I would return to pray, "Lord, I'm willing to give up Mary, if it's Your will, but PLEASE DON'T TAKE HER AWAY!"

On the second day of the fast, while at a fellow student's home, I slipped into his bedroom to pray. Again, I cried out, "Lord, I'm willing to give up Mary, if it's Your will, but PLEASE DON'T TAKE HER AWAY!"

At that very moment, I received revelation knowledge from God. He brought to my attention that I was in Bible College, preparing for ministry to seek to win souls to Him. Yet, I was letting a temporary earthly relationship with a girl outweigh the eternal value of the soul of Rick. I saw it!

I repented of that selfishness. I knew a sinner's soul carried infinite value. I no longer fought to keep Mary. I left her and our relationship in the hands of God. Then, I rushed to the kitchen to get something to eat! The matter was settled in my heart. However, to my delight, Mary realized that she was hoping for something that was not to be. She gave up on her task with Rick, and we soon resumed dating.

In retrospect, I see that God was developing the heart of an evangelist in this future evangelist. Similarly, if you will "do the work of an evangelist," He also wants to reveal to you the incomparable value of the soul of even just one lost sinner.

Dating Mary once again, we spent even more time together. Whenever I was tempted to commit some serious sin or to quit the Bible College, I thought of Mary and was afraid that God might punish my evil by taking her out of my life! I now see that God used Mary as a prop for the theater of my life while the drama continued to unfold.

We started dating every Friday night, then Saturday nights too. On Sundays, I picked her up and we drove to her church, the Anaheim Foursquare Church. After the morning service, we usually spent all afternoon doing fun things together and went back for the Crusader's hour at 6:00 PM, before the 7:00 evening service. After church, we parked for a while near her house, then I took her home and drove back to college to beat the 10:00 PM student curfew. That was the routine then. It's the…

"Tale as old as time: Beauty and the… Bible College Student!"

With Mary going to church.

I became an active part of Mary's church. I had never been baptized in water, so our pastor baptized me. Since I was a Bible College student preparing for ministry, the adult sponsor who led the youth group appointed me as President. I guess they figured I must have leadership skills, but I was a terrible president! In junior high, I was the school president in the 8th grade. However, the vice-principal said I was, "the worst president in the history of the school." I was NOT one of those "born leaders."

Mary and I often arrived late for the youth service. We had so much fun together that we neglected the time. When we arrived, I often burst through the door full of energy, but totally unprepared to help lead the youth. The adult sponsor usually had to take the reins for the service. The pastor once asked me to lead the song service for morning worship. As I led the hymns, waving my arms, I glanced back at Mary. She was busting up laughing at me. Well, seeing that, I couldn't control my laughter. So, throughout the song service, I kept trying to lead while trying not to laugh. The pastor NEVER asked me to lead the service again!

I am living proof of 1 Corinthians 1:26, 27 which reads, "Not many wise according to the flesh...are called, but God has chosen the foolish things of the world..." When Donald Trump was unexpectedly elected President in 2016, my wife said to me afterward, "Dea, if a man like Donald Trump could be elected President, there is hope for you." Thus, my fellow foolish evangelists, there is hope for you too! God likes our kind of ilk!

Sometimes, Mary and I drove up to the San Antonio Dam, one of the favorite hangouts for dating teens from Chaffey High School. Rock-and-roll blared from my car radio back in the days before cassette, 8 track, CD's, or Bluetooth. Teens switched between local radio stations KRLA and KFWB.

With rock-and-roll pulsating in our ears, my arm wrapped around Mary, peering down at the thousands of lights in the cities below the dam, I felt like a king! I waved my arm toward the brightly lit valley below and boasted, "Mary, see those lights? That's our world!" I idealistically considered that world below as a personal challenge to conquer with Mary at my side!

I firmly believed I would one day marry Mary, though she was just a sophomore in high school and I was a freshman in college. My love for Mary grew. Meanwhile, however, God had another girl in mind for me to marry. He also had an infinitely more important love for me to develop, a love for lost souls!

Within all my running around and having fun, Pastor Jack Hayford, a 32-year-old LIFE professor at the time, entered my life. He soon was my favorite teacher. He had not yet become pastor of The Church on the Way in Van Nuys, California. Nor was he a nationally respected leader and songwriter. At the time we met, he had hitherto not written the song "Majesty" nor authored fifty-five books. He wasn't famous yet, and I, at the time, had no idea he would soon become the most important influence in my life. I would within months be shot out of a canon!

Rev. Jack W. Hayford, B.Th.

Orientation, Journalism
Personal Evangelism

Pastor Hayford taught a class called Personal Evangelism. That two-unit course was to set the pace for my future ministry. Seeking to instill in us our responsibility as leaders to preach the Word as a lifestyle, with a primary goal of winning souls to Christ, Jack taught us from a now out-of-print book. He walked us through a step-by-step method of sharing the gospel and required us to memorize the opening questions to start a conversation, the Scriptures to quote, and some good illustrations to use.

Jack required us to memorize author C.S. Lovett's entire technique referred to as the Encounter Method. On the final exam, we had to write out, from memory, that entire gospel presentation. All these years later in 2020, I pulled from my file my official college transcript and saw an "A" in that Personal Evangelism class. I am so glad I thoroughly learned and memorized a tool for effective evangelism! How it changed my life! (See Chapter 19 to learn the Encounter Method).

Not long after being "equipped ... for the work of the ministry" (Ephesians 4:8-11), I experienced my first opportunity to use the Encounter Method. One sunny Southern California morning, while on my way to pick up Mary and attend church, I noticed a hitchhiker and pulled over to give him a ride. We talked a little, and he told me he was a Marine. As we drove, I thought to myself, "This is a good opportunity to use what Jack taught us."

I led the conversation, as ALL soul-winners must. In over half-a-century, I have never had someone walk up to me and say, "Tell me, please! What must I do to be saved?" The proud Marine listened carefully, and he politely answered my questions. He continued to listen as I quoted Revelation 3:20, the suggested final appeal in the gospel presentation I had learned from Jack, "I stand at the door and knock. If anyone hears my voice and opens the door I will come into him." Then came the all-important punch line, "Would you like to open the door of your heart to Christ?" He immediately affirmed that he did.

I could hardly believe it! What! You, me, here, now? But it was really happening. Thus, I led my first soul to Christ. Oh, the joy that flooded my soul!

During that same week, I picked up a couple of hippy-types hitchhiking on Sunset Boulevard. I shared the gospel with them, carefully guiding the conversation as I drove. After stopping at their destination in downtown Hollywood, I asked them both, "Would you like to receive Christ?" One said, "No." The other said, "Yes." I requested that the uninterested man please leave the car, and then I led the other man to Christ; the second soul in one week! Oh, the joy that flooded my soul!

As soon as I returned to my dorm room, I knelt at my bunk and prayed one of the most important prayers I have ever prayed:

"Lord, this is wonderful leading souls to Christ. I want to do this for the rest of my life. So, give me no peace until I am doing my best to win souls for You."

God began to answer that prayer in an extraordinary way.

The Lord poured into the heart of that 17-year-old a zeal to win the lost. Soul-winning became my passion. I passed out tracts and witnessed, even walked up to total strangers to share the gospel day-after-day. I loved doing the work of an evangelist!

One time, Mary and I were driving around when I noticed two girls walking down the street. I stopped the car. We ran over to the girls and I asked them, "Have you heard about the invasion from outer space?" They incredulously asked, "What invasion?" I replied, "Jesus is coming!" After I explained the gospel way to prepare for His coming, they accepted Christ. The next day, one of the girls came with us to church!

I started visiting relatives and old friends, seeking specifically to win them to Christ. I attended some teen-parties and started preaching to entire living rooms full of lost souls! This effort became THE driving force in my life!

I stopped dating Mary on Friday nights because that became my official, "Soul-winning night!" I went to places like Taco Bell and passed out tracts to the outside diners. I remember stopping by a teen dance and patiently waiting outside for someone to exit for a cigarette. Then, I hit them with both barrels of the gospel shotgun! I was doing my best to win souls to the Lord!

Mary and I still dated, as usual, on Saturday nights. We drove up to the dam again, but the world had become a very different place for me. The same rock-and-roll shrieked from the radio. The same arm wrapped around the same girl. But as I scanned the lights below us, I no longer saw them as representing a world to conquer for a girl. I saw those lights, not as shining points of glory, but rather, as representing thousands of eternal souls that would one day be screaming in the flames of hell!

One Saturday afternoon, as Mary and I headed once more for the dam, our fun was interrupted by a hitchhiker whom I felt compelled to stop and pick up. I witnessed to him and talked at length with him about the Lord, even pulling to the side of the road so we could talk better. After he left the car, we took off again. Down the road a little way, another lost soul awaited me. I stopped for him and dedicated some time to discuss his relationship with God. By the time we finished talking and I'd let him out, it was really too late to keep heading towards the mountains. As we headed back towards Anaheim, Mary let me know her displeasure at missing out on her anticipated personal time with me. She was disappointed, but I was appointed -- appointed to be a preacher of the gospel and a witness for the Lord!

Not long after that, as usual, I picked Mary up for a Saturday night date. As we drove away from her house, I remembered someone I had led to Christ and was concerned about how he was doing spiritually. I stopped at a phone booth and gave him a call to encourage him in the faith. When I returned to the car, Mary greeted me with, "Dea, I don't think it's fair that you do the Lord's work on our dates."

Mary's words were the handwriting on the wall. The Lord was making it clear to both of us that our future marriage was NOT a marriage made in heaven. She did not carry the same calling as me and was not patient or willing to make the same sacrifices that I had been called to make. Towards the end of the school year, Mary decided to break up with me. I still can picture myself parked out in front of Knott's Berry Farm, near her house, eating carrot sticks and drinking Bubble Up while crying like a baby. Mary breaking up with me was the saddest day of my life up to that juncture.

For weeks I often thought about Mary and felt butterflies in my stomach. Alfred Lord Tennyson once wrote, "Tis better to have loved and lost, than never to have loved at all." That so-called "Lord" obviously knew nothing about love, at least not my love for a girl named Mary!

But life goes on, and the Spring Term came to a close. I moved back in with my parents for the summer and continued driving to downtown Los Angeles where I worked as a janitor for the Full Gospel Business Men's Fellowship International (FGBMFI).

There was no further reason to attend Mary's church. Whenever I attended, I just sadly sat in a different row from Mary. So, I decided to visit other churches. I continued watching for souls to lead to the Lord while also looking for another soulmate! Without warning, my life was about to take a dramatic turn as I entered my first great trial which I share in the next chapter.

The Wisdom to Win Souls

Ponder and consider this: I never won a soul to Christ until I was specifically taught how to do so by Jack Hayford.

To do something, you first must know how to do it. Firemen must learn how to extinguish fires. Likewise, soul-winners must learn how to witness effectively to extinguish the fires of hell. I was taught that an effective soul-winner needs to have a plan, Scriptures memorized, illustrations, leading questions, and other tools ready to "do the work of an evangelist."

"He who wins souls is wise" (Proverbs 11:30).

We can learn two corollaries from this verse.

First, it is wise to be about the business of soul-winning. My life was wrapped up in a love affair with a girl until God showed me what is really important in life -- preparing for eternity.

Second, we need wisdom to win souls. I will share with you some of the wisdom God has given me: wisdom from God, wisdom from Jack Hayford, wisdom from other teachers and writers, and the increase of wisdom that comes to every Christian in the school of experience, one from which we never graduate.

You have read thus far hopefully because you are wise enough to realize you need to know more about evangelists and evangelism. As you continue reading, I will share many of my thrilling experiences in the science of an evangelistic focused ministry. In later chapters, you'll find many resources: books, websites, and tracts, to add to your wisdom for soul-winning.

Read on, wise student!

6

MY FIRST GREAT TRIAL

"The Lord disciplines everyone he loves. He severely disciplines everyone he accepts as his child. My child, pay attention when the Lord disciplines you. Don't give up when he corrects you" (Hebrews 12:5, 6 GW).

Early on, I struggled with obedience as a Christian. God was very patient with me. He must really love me too because He surely spanked me through the years! The Bible tells us, "Whom the Lord loves He chastens" (Hebrews 12:6). The first actual spanking I felt He gave me occurred while I was still dating Mary. Driving to our church in my VW one rainy Sunday morning, a sensation began swelling up within me. The best way to describe it is a feeling of rebellion. As the rock-and-roll music roared, I felt the flesh crying out to manifest itself. The sinful nature can feel so good! I wanted to "enjoy the pleasures of sin for a season" (Hebrews 10:25).

Suddenly, my car began to slide back and forth on the freeway. It was scary, but I corrected the drifting motion and got back safely in my lane. "Did God cause that to get my attention?" Soon I was again cruising at 65mph in one of the most dangerous cars in history. I regained my composure and enjoyed listening to my music, still reveling in that cool feeling of rebellion.

Without warning, my car drifted again, this time turning completely around as it slid down the I-5 freeway. My door swung wide open as the vehicle came to a stop on the shoulder while I gripped the steering wheel. This time, I knew God was chastening me! I put my seat belt on (nobody wore seat belts back then). I buckled up (just in case God had any bright ideas of killing me that day). Then, I carefully drove the rest of the way to church. At the altar call, I fell on my knees, cried and repented before God for being such a rebel. I felt relief. But, had I learned my lesson yet? Apparently not, as I soon entered the greatest trial of my life.

LIFE Bible College required all students to turn in a "Weekly Christian Service Report" to the school office every Monday. On the form, students reported which services we attended and any special things we did in those services. Then the form asked, "How many people did you witness to this week?" followed by, "How many souls did you lead to Christ?" It was not unusual for me to report that I won a number of souls to Christ that week.

Students simply left their completed report in a basket at the window of the office. Sometimes while turning in my report, if no staff members were watching, I flipped through the stack to see what other students reported. I was tickled that usually, I was about the only one who had witnessed to ANYONE that week. I was even happier if I had been the only one who had led someone to Christ. I felt so proud in the knowledge that I was so much more spiritual than the other students!

I read books about great soul-winners of the past for inspiration and tips on how I could be more effective in my witness. One day, while walking near the parking lot next to the office where I worked, I gleefully thought, "You are a great soul-winner. You are probably right up there with some of the great soul-winners like Moody and Torrey. In fact, you may be,

The Greatest Soul-Winner of all Time!

Satan filled my heart with pride just as he filled Ananias' heart with a lie in Acts 5:3. The Lord had seen enough. He had to deal with His son, and He knew exactly how to do it. A short time afterward, while I was at work cleaning a pastor's office, a word came to mind that I heard recently, gluttony. I casually asked the pastor, "What does the word gluttony mean?"

He replied, "Overeating."

As I continued sweeping, I thought to myself, "I eat an awful lot of food." In fact, I have actually won five eating contests. I enjoyed a lightning-fast metabolism and loved to eat. I told myself, "I've got to start eating less. I certainly don't want to be a glutton."

Students who lived in the dorms ate in the college cafeteria. Meals were buffet style, and we could eat all we wanted, breakfast, lunch, and dinner. As I walked through the line that very night, I decided to eat less than usual. I filled my plate, but not too full. I sat down and plowed through that little pile of grub quickly, and I was still hungry.

I glanced over at the buffet but quickly turned my head. "No, I don't want to be a glutton!" Then, I peered longingly toward the smells beckoning me to visit again. "Get behind me Satan!" I cried. My will-power spent, my hunger pains crying, "Feed me!" I returned to the buffet line and refilled my plate.

After finishing my second helping, I felt so guilty. Inside my mind, I rebuked myself, "I am a glutton!" But then I thought, "Well if I am going to be a glutton, I might as well be a good one." I returned to the buffet line for even more food. Afterward, I felt even more terrible!

At the midweek service, during the altar call, I repented, knelt, and asked God to forgive me, making a determination to not overeat again. However, the next morning, the cafeteria served pancakes! I love pancakes, you know, the kind dripping with butter and lots of syrup! I hesitantly and timidly put a short stack on my plate and finished them in no time. I gazed longingly towards the buffet.

"No!" I demanded of myself. "I will not be a glutton," turning my head away from the temptation. But soon, like a magnet, my attention fixated on the hot, steaming flapjacks, enticing me as though saying, "Eat me!"

"Get behind me Satan!" I whispered to an unseen foe.

My will-power again spent, I returned for more pancakes! Stuffed with quickly devoured pancakes and full of condemnation for my iniquity, there was no doubt about it now. I was a glutton.

After gaining 20 pounds!

Thus, began the first great trial of my life, the compulsion to overeat. Food, I discovered, was everywhere! At some party or get-together, my first priority became to find any available snacks. At times, I would stuff myself until my stomach felt sick. I even stuck my finger down my throat to try to regurgitate. Apparently, I have a poor vomiting reflex and never could make myself throw up, though maybe gag a little. In retrospect, I think the Lord protected me from bulimia before most of us even knew it existed!

I began to gain weight. Soon I ballooned 20 pounds heavier, which at 18-years of age and with my fast metabolism would be like many people gaining 200 pounds! Often, I walked by the candy bar machine at college, and impulsively bought a candy bar. They only cost a dime back then. I even remember when a candy bar only cost a nickel. I still remember one day eating only half of the candy bar and getting so disgusted with myself that I threw the other half off of the 5th story roof!

Another time, I went with some other LIFE students to an ice cream parlor in downtown Hollywood. We each got our cones with our favorite flavors. As we stepped out of the store to the sidewalk, I glanced down at my ice cream. Suddenly, that pile of scrumptious fat and sugar became my tormenting enemy. I loudly cussed and slammed the ice cream to the sidewalk. In shock, the students ran quickly to the car to get away from me. They thought I had flipped! Afterward, I felt sullen and was obviously sorry for doing such an un-Christlike thing. They finally, relieved, let me back into the car. I wish I could say it ended there, but it didn't.

A guest speaker was coming to a friend's church. She told me the speaker had a deliverance ministry. I went, hoping. When he invited people for prayer, I came forward. After telling him about my battle with food, he responded, matter-of-factly, "You have 14 demons of gluttony and I'm going to cast them out." It sounded like a good idea to me, so I submitted to his prayer. That guy did not do me a bit of good! Right after the service, I drove to the 7-11 market and bought a pie, ice cream, and a candy bar.

During this great trial, I witnessed to people far less often. I lived under such condemnation that I felt unworthy to witness for Christ. What a hypocrite! Who was I to tell others about the peace and power of following the Lord, when I felt so little peace and so little power?

Being spiritually weak, I begin to flirt with sin. Mary was gone, so the fear of losing her no longer served as a restraining force. One Friday, I decided to back-slide for the night, thinking to myself that I would just repent afterward. The devil isn't very original, is he?

I cashed my weekly paycheck, took my weekly shower, and headed for Hollywood. I don't remember what exactly I planned for the night; maybe see a movie. When I applied for LIFE, I gave my word I wouldn't attend theaters. Maybe I planned to go to a bar and, though underage, try to get a cocktail or two.

I do remember that on this night of backsliding, I could not think of a better way to start it all off than with a double-scoop, hot-fudge sundae! I parked outside the same ice cream parlor where I had my fit, ordered my dessert, quickly gobbled it down, and then headed back to my car with an attitude like,

"Lookout Hollywood! Here comes the backslider!"

When I walked outside, I immediately discovered: MY CAR WAS GONE! Frantically scanning the area, I saw a tow truck driver nearby preparing to tow away another car. I ran up to him and asked him what was going on. He pointed to a sign, "No Parking. Tow Away Zone." Crestfallen, I asked, "Well, where is my car?" He said, "Hop in my truck, and I'll take you."

I forked over $25.00 to get my car out of the Los Angeles Police garage and drove away like a whipped puppy. Now broke, I knew for sure that this was the chastening of the Lord. As a result, I repented and then walked the streets of Hollywood passing out tracts and preaching the gospel as good Bible College student should!

Unfortunately, some Christians don't learn their lesson the first time, and I undoubtedly was one of those, often, way too often!

Another night, I decided to go dancing. I needed a girlfriend again and learned in high school that dances provided one of the best venues to meet girls. When I applied to LIFE, I also promised not to attend dances. However, that particular night, I decided that I would just ask God to forgive me later. I made sure to choose a dance far enough away from the Bible College or the town where I attended church so that no one would see me. I read about a dance in Riverside, maybe 60 miles from LIFE, and 20 miles from my church. That sounded safe enough to me.

Not in the mood to sin all by myself that night, I called up my high school friend, Kenny Johnstone, to invite him along. He agreed, and we drove to the dance together in his car. He lit up a cigarette. I didn't smoke, but, hey, if smoking was a sin, I wanted to do it. Before long, we both enjoyed smoking and listening to rock-and-roll on our way to a night of fleshly pleasures.

We stopped at a light in Riverside, and another group of youth pulled up next to us. As the light turned green, both cars sped off in a drag race. Kenny won the race, but we noticed out the rear window that a cop had turned on his lights and pulled the other driver over. We roared with laughter at their plight. But, we stopped laughing when another cop pulled into view behind us with his red lights on. Kenny got his first ticket that night. I should have realized it was also the first sign that it was not a good night to sin, but I didn't heed the warning.

Kenny and I continued our quest and soon arrived at the dance. We enjoyed dancing, talking to girls, and generally having fun, until a girl walked up to me with a shocked look on her face. Cupping her hand over her mouth, she asked, "Are you, Dea Warford?" I never was a good liar. I admitted that I was he.

The girl said she remembered me from Camp Cedar Crest that summer where I had visited between my freshman and sophomore year of college. She probably saw me at the camp praying for kids, testifying, and maybe counseling some.

I had been found out! The Lord chastened the backslider again. Immediately, I walked over to a sofa against the wall and knelt down to repent and beg God to forgive me once more. Then, I found Kenny and told him I couldn't stay any longer and had to go home. He honored my request.

How I dreaded going back to school that week. I just knew that the girl who caught me would spread the evil report about me. People would hear how I was out dancing instead of kneeling at the altar with repentant youths. I waited with bated breath for Dean Clarence Hall to call me to his office to give an account for the bad report which would surely reach him soon. Yet, he never called and no one at the school ever mentioned it.

A little later, though, word got back to me through the grapevine that someone saw me at a dance. However, the person reported that I was seen, "Passing out tracts and witnessing."

Hallelujah! God saw my repentant heart that evening and forgave me. He even allowed a false rumor to spare his son, reminiscent of the false rumor that the Lord used to save Hezekiah from his enemies (2 Kings 19:7). Talk about undeserved grace! However, this was one chastening I had learned from. I never smoked or went dancing again!

Nevertheless, I continued to struggle with overeating and the resultant condemnation. I sought counseling and prayer, but the battle was ongoing. Then, in the spring of my sophomore year, I took a class on "The Book of Romans." Dr. Leslie Eno, a wonderful teacher, led the class, verse by verse, explaining the intent of Paul the Apostle's words. Something significant, a catharsis of sorts, a metamorphosis, took place in my soul.

The enlightenment didn't happen overnight, but as I studied day-by-day, I began understanding the glorious truths of our justification by faith. Truths such as Romans 5:1-5 and 8:1-4 began to transform my heart. I realized that although my weight and health might be determined by how many calories I ate, my relationship with God was not! The peace of God began to settle on my soul. The power of God's Word worked powerfully in me.

"Therefore, having been justified by faith, we have peace with God through our Lord Jesus Christ, through whom also we have access by faith into this grace in which we stand" (Romans 5:1, 2).

I found myself progressively eating less. Instead of two or three pieces of pie, I ate only one. One serving was enough. My preoccupation with food was gone. The excess weight was soon gone. My soul was restored with a sense of joy and authority.

"There is therefore now no condemnation to those who are in Christ Jesus, who do not walk according to the flesh, but according to the Spirit" (Romans 8:1).

The Lord delivered me from condemnation, from overeating, and from any invisible demons of gluttony who might have been trying to take advantage of me in my ignorance (2 Corinthians 2:11). My "gluttony" struggle was indeed overeating and I was too preoccupied with food, for sure.

Now, I know that there is not a precise line of demarcation for gluttony: a weight of food or a certain number of calories which if you exceed that standard you are a glutton. This sin should be individualized between a man, his meal, and his Messiah.

That was a tough, challenging, and frustrating period in my life. The self-proclaimed "greatest soul-winner of all time" had been unveiled as the great sinner that he was. As a result, I was a humbled man, not necessarily humble, mind you, but humbled.

I passed the test, at least well enough that God continued His call on my life, and I wasn't kicked out of LIFE either! Though God would have to correct me often through my many years in His service, this was the year that stands out as the first, longest, and possibly the most difficult of them all. It's funny to think and write about it all now, but it certainly wasn't funny then!

Warning!

When you do the work of an evangelist and start seeing results, take it from me: DON'T GET A BIG HEAD!

The Bible specifically tells us, "Pride goes before destruction, and a haughty spirit before a fall" (Proverbs 16:18). Satan was thrown out of heaven because of his pride (Isaiah 14 and Ezekiel 28). Nebuchadnezzar was thrown into an insane asylum, or the equivalent, because of pride (Daniel 5:28-37). Because of David's pride, 70,000 people died (1 Chronicles 21).

People go to hell because of pride!

Pride puffs us up to the point that God cannot use us nearly as much as He desires to, as I learned the hard way. Pride keeps us from witnessing because of the fear of rejection. Also, consider this: doesn't working those extra hours to acquire nice things; cars, clothes, etc., "the pride of life," keep us busy in activities other than soul-winning? (See 1 John 2:16)

Consider this: Paul became one of the greatest soul-winners of all time, yet God kept him humble by a lifetime of great trials as shown in 2 Corinthians 11:23-30; 12:5-10. Paul wants us to realize that we should seek to be successful soul-winners, Yet always, always give the Lord the glory for any accomplishments.

"…what have you that has not been given to you? But if it has been given to you, what cause have you for pride, as if it had not been given to you?" (1 Corinthians 4:7).

Use your God-given gifts humbly, always mindful of Who they came from! Evangelism is one of the highest forms of spiritual warfare. You don't believe me? Announce a special door to door soul-winning endeavor and see how many show up! Satan fights attempts to snatch souls from his claws. He fights it with all his evil heart. If God begins using you in evangelism, you will become a special threat to the kingdom of darkness. Expect a counterattack!

Early on, the enemy used my sins against me again and again as I walked the sawdust trail. A natural propensity to be legalistic, perhaps because of my exposure as a child to a very strict and demanding church, became a great weapon against me. The enemy demanded me to keep a strict diet. Then, when I failed, he demanded that I walk in condemnation. My natural selfishness, stubbornness, and disobedience also helped make his work easy.

God used me in spite of these sins, and He'll use you in spite of yours too. He used Moses even with his great anger. He used David even with his murderous and lustful heart. He used Paul in spite of his pride. He used Peter in spite of his denial of Christ. God even spoke through a jackass in the Bible! He spoke through me, a very imperfect evangelist, and He wants to speak through you also, the imperfect vessel that you are!

As family members encouraged me in writing, a relative told me to entitle this book, "A Great Soul-Winner." I could not do that because I am, unequivocally, NOT a great soul-winner. I do hope heaven at least considers me a soul-winner. I know any rewards that might possibly be coming to me in heaven, I will cast humbly at Jesus' feet because whether great or small, He alone deserves the glory for anything you or I might be enabled to accomplish.

"Whoever speaks must speak God's words. Whoever serves must serve with the strength God supplies so that in every way God receives glory through Jesus Christ. Glory and power belong to Jesus Christ forever and ever! Amen" (1 Peter 4:11 GW).

In the following chapters, I will share some of my soul-winning encounters. I genuinely hope that as a result of this book…

Heaven will consider you a "soul-winner."

7

MY FIRST MINISTRY: TEENAGERS

"After all, what gives us hope and joy, and what will be our proud reward and crown as we stand before our Lord Jesus when he returns? It is you" (1 Thessalonians 2:19 NLT).

At the beginning of the fall semester of my sophomore year, I moved back into the dorms. I continued working at FGBMFI and began attending a church in Long Beach where a girl I met at camp attended. An important change in my life soon took place.

I preached at a church, and my mother came to hear her 18-year-old boy in action. She was backslidden for many years, but answered my altar call and got back in relationship with the Lord. We both knew she needed a home church. Every new convert does! She also carried a deep concern about me commuting over 40 miles to that church in Long Beach. The Lord was about to take care of us both in a beautiful way.

One day, at the FGBMFI office, a workmate asked me for a favor. She had a real estate sign that she borrowed from a friend who lived in Ontario. She asked if I could return it when I went back home for the weekend to be with my parents, as I usually did. I enjoyed mom's home-cooking and allowed her the privilege of doing a week's worth of my dirty laundry. I put the sign in my car and after work headed out to join the heavy L.A. weekend traffic.

When I arrived at the house to leave their sign, I was greeted at the door by, "Dea!" Two teens, I had met at summer camp now surprised me. I stood at their front porch. They invited me in to visit awhile and told me that the youth leader at their home church recently resigned. They attended the Upland Foursquare Church in the adjacent city and encouraged me to apply for the position.

When I shared this with my mom, she said that if I started attending the church, she would join me and attend also. Concerned for her soul, I arranged to meet the pastor, Vivian Twyford. After talking together and seeing my burden for the lost, and my movie star looks, she offered me the position. Soon I stepped in as the youth leader, a position which I maintained for the next three-and-a-half years. This became a very eventful time in my life. The youth group grew rapidly. We also created a gospel choir and took close to 50 teenagers to Camp Cedar Crest.

Teaching those youths in Sunday School and often preaching to them at our Sunday evening "Crusader" youth service at 6 PM, before the 7 PM evening service, polished my speaking and sermon organization skills. I led many quite a few teens to Christ and discipled them to following Him. I also taught them how to share the gospel step-by-step just as Jack Hayford previously taught me.

After training the youth group in evangelism, I told them that they could win their classmates to the Lord right on their high school campuses. One of the girls, Charlotte, who a few years later became my sister-in-law, came up to me after a session and reproved me, "Dea, you can't lead people to Christ at school!" She then proceeded to explain all the reasons she felt it couldn't be done. I responded, "Yes you can lead souls to Christ at school!" Convincing an evangelist otherwise would be quite a task for anyone!

The next service, Charlotte joyfully came up to me and said, "Dea, you were right, you can lead souls to Christ at school!" She then grabbed the hand of a boy following her to introduce him to me. She led him to Christ while she was seated next to him in the school library.

While kneeling at the altar after Sister Twyford preached, I experienced the joy of leading a teenager, Bob Brazell to Christ. Later, Bob was at a house party for teens where I also had been invited. After the usual party festivities, I suggested that we turn out the lights, and I would tell a spooky story. They all agreed. My imaginative mind made the story as hair-raising as possible.

Then, I abruptly changed the narrative, "Now, I am going to tell you a true story." With that, I described the horrific events of the book of Revelation. I spoke of the wars, the famine, the pestilences, and the blood as high as the horse's bridle with a brief explanation of how to be saved. After I felt they were adequately warned, I asked for the lights to be turned back on and then asked, "How many of you want to receive Christ and escape all these terrible events?" Several did, and I prayed with them.

I taught Charlotte how to do the work of an evangelist. But Bob "caught" how to do it. At Bob's next high school house party, after the usual party festivities, he suggested that they turn out the lights, and he'd tell a spooky story. They agreed to do so. He improvised a frightening story and made it as hair-raising as he could. Then, he abruptly changed the narrative, "Now, I am going to tell you a true story."

Bob and his wife, Cathy, whom he met in the Upland youth group.

With that, Bob described the horrific events of the book of Revelation. He spoke of the wars, the famine, the pestilences, and the blood as high as the horse's bridle with a brief explanation of how to be saved. He requested that the lights be turned back on and asked, "How many of you want to receive Christ and escape all these terrible events?" Several did, and he prayed with them.

Valerie, one of the teenage girls saved through Bob at the party, started attending our church. Years later, while I held a revival at a church in Cottonwood, Northern California, Valerie sat in the congregation. After the service, we spoke, and she shared that she was now married, but her Christian husband had been in a paralyzing car accident, and was now confined to a wheelchair. He blamed God for his problems and stopped attending church.

I asked if I could visit Valerie's husband, and she was happy to have me do so. I pointed out to him that he was blaming the wrong person. The devil was behind his suffering and everyone else's suffering in this fallen world. I promised him that God loves him and can redeem his circumstance. Convinced, he repented and came back to the Lord that day!

I was Bob Brazell's father in the faith. Valerie was Bob's daughter in the faith and my grand-daughter in the faith. Now, her husband was my great-grandson in the faith. This is God's plan for everyone. One person can start a spiritual domino effect that continually rescues the perishing in an ever-expanded circle of influence. But it always, ALWAYS, begins with one. You can be that one, the first cause of entire families entering the kingdom.

Our youth group hosted an evangelistic outreach one Halloween, called a "Horrorthon." I knew virtually nothing about the demonic world at the time, but I knew a little about soul-winning. God, aware of my youthful innocence, and in His grace used the event anyway, in spite of its name! We utilized an old field with an old barn on a ranch in the somewhat undeveloped farmlands of Southern Ontario. As a child, I played in that same barn while my dad observed gang cockfights, somewhat hidden from the peering eyes of the police. The youth group and I built a pretty cool walk-through "House of Terror". Prior to the event, the local Daily Report newspaper sent a reporter to take pictures which provided us some good, free advertising. I also rented a gorilla suit and wore it while standing on the corner outside Chaffey High School handing out flyers inviting youth to the "Horrorthon." A pretty fair crowd came out that night, and we put on quite a show. Then, near the end of the food, skits, etc. I stood up and preached the gospel.

Around thirty youth responded and stepped forward to receive Christ. One of the boys, Clayton George, joined our youth group. However, after he was absent for a few weeks, I went to call on him at his house. He apparently felt offended at something, and when I urged him to come back to the church, he responded, "I would rather be dead!"

The next Sunday, during our evening service, our youth group sat in our usual area of the sanctuary. Pastor Twyford walked out very sullenly and announced that Clayton George's father had just called. Clayton was in a rock-climbing accident that Sunday and tragically fell to his death. Youth cried and grieved as their fantasy world of fun and games abruptly came to a halt.

The grim reality of death shocked them with the truth that even teenagers are not exempt from tragedy. There are few things in this world as "cruel as the grave" (Song of Solomon 8:6 KJV).

Above: Teens watching a movie at the Horrorthon, and below, I am giving an altar call, asking those making a decision to come forward.

I hope to see Clayton in heaven. I have good reason for that hope too! Paul wrote in 1 Corinthians 11:30-32, "For this reason...many sleep (are dead). When we are judged, we are chastened by the Lord, that we may not be condemned (to hell) with the world." Thank God for this truth.

How much better it is to be "chastened by the Lord," die at 15, but enter heaven, than to live 95 years to only die and then enter the lake of fire.

I have a long list of sinners that I pray for daily.

I truly would like to see all of them happy, in church, and living productive lives. But, as an evangelist, my one overruling burden is that they are ready to die and will ultimately escape hell.

Clayton's death was one of my saddest experiences while serving as a youth minister. Thankfully, many joyful events occurred as well.

One of my favorites took place while I worked a part-time job selling shoes at J.C. Penney's in Ontario. A woman came in with her two teenage daughters. She and I talked alone for a moment. She said she was a Christian, but her two daughters were not.

I kept my eye on those two cute girls until the family left the store. Driving home that night after work, thinking again about those girls, I suddenly felt an unusually deep burden in my heart for their souls. The burden was so compelling that I cried out loud for God to save them! More about them in a moment...

The summer before my last year of Bible College, our youth group hosted a social at a park. Someone invited Grant Hollist, a teen from Alta Loma High School, to join us. He had just graduated from high school where he was the class president-elect his senior year and a varsity football quarterback/end. His dad was a Bishop in a Mormon Church, but his mom was a Christian.

Grant planned to attend college but wasn't sure where. He was also unsure about many aspects of his spiritual life. The Lord was working on his behalf.

Grant Hollist, Treasurer

When Grant drove into the parking lot to attend our gathering, I walked up to his car and started talking with him. He told me he was a Mormon and didn't want to join our social gathering. We conversed a while longer, and as he was leaving, I gave him my card and said, "When you want to know the errors of Mormonism and truth of real Christianity, call me."

Two days later, Grant called and was ready to talk with me. That evening, I drove to the service station where he worked. Between Grant stepping out from time-to-time to fill a car with gas, we sat together at an office desk. Already having researched Mormonism at some length, in the back of my Bible, I wrote the key doctrines of their church and the Scriptures that proved the falsehood of those doctrines. Half-a-century later, in the back of my present Bible, I still have that same list I compiled about Mormonism. In chapter 22, I have listed those same doctrines and Scriptures to help you in witnessing to Mormons and another list for dealing with Jehovah's Witnesses.

When the time came for Grant to close the business for the day, he didn't have a ride home that night, so I offered to give him a lift. I soon pulled over to the side of the road and asked, "What about it Grant. Would you like to receive Christ?" He answered, "Yes." I usually lead people in a prayer, but for some reason, I told him, "Just pray out loud and in your own words ask the Lord to come into your heart."

Grant bowed his head and in the customary Mormon fashion with a dignified tone of voice began praying, "Father in heaven, I ask that Your

Son Jesus would come into my heart." Grant's voice grew louder. "And I can feel him coming inside." At a faster pace and now with shaking and gesturing his arms, he prayed, "He's in me now. I can feel it." I had never seen anything like it in my life. It was one of the most glorious conversions I'd ever witnessed.

Grant and I discovered that we had a mutual friend, Stan, who happened to be a member of the Upland Foursquare Church. Excitedly, we immediately drove to Stan's house and began banging on his door. Grant greeted the rudely awakened man with the good news of how he had gotten saved. We went inside and in our friend's kitchen, the three of us lifted our hands toward heaven giving all thanks and praise to God for His great salvation.

Grant became a bold witness for Christ. He won another teenager to the Lord who joined our youth group. Grant's life changed quickly. He decided he wanted to go to Bible college with me! He moved in with my family. My sister who also decided to go to LIFE was a junior. I was a senior, and Grant was a freshman. That fall, we drove to school together.

I shared my bedroom with my new disciple, and we even shared a double bed. (Young people, this was at a time in America when nobody thought anything of two men sleeping in the same bed). One night, just before I drifted off to sleep, I felt Grant's strong quarterback arm wrap around me, and he told me the sweetest words I have ever heard,

"Thanks, Dea, for leading me to Christ."

This reminded me of another experience. One of my first revivals as a twenty-two-year-old traveling evangelist occurred in Johannesburg, California, which was at one time a thriving little mining town in the desert but by then had only a population of around 300. The first night the revival meeting included just me, the pastor and his wife, and three other persons. By the last night of the revival, maybe 30 attended.

One teenage boy, a Jehovah's Witness, accepted Christ during the crusade. As I paced back and forth praying around the altar after a service, he knelt at the altar again in prayer. Suddenly, so filled with joy at his newly found salvation, and without wasting the time to even stand to his feet, he literally crawled towards me with his two arms outstretched to embrace me and cried,

"Thank you!"

Hallelujah! Can you understand why this writer is so enthusiastic about soul-winning?

Before closing this chapter, I must add the finishing touch to the above story about Grant. A few days after he accepted the Lord, I drove to his house to follow-up on my new convert. Please know that Grant lived in a highly populated suburb with many tens of thousands of people. So, it was much more than mere coincidence that when I knocked on his door, Grant answered it saying, "I want you to meet my sisters," and there, standing behind Grant in the entryway, stood two teenage girls. They were the same girls from the shoe store and for whom God gave me such a strong burden for their souls that I cried out to Him for their salvation.

Soon, we all sat in their den, and I shared the gospel with Grant's sisters. With tears in their eyes, they both knelt at the sofa and came to Christ. Years later, I was preaching in a church not many miles from their house. One of those girls read that I was going to be in town and came to hear me. Imagine my delight to discover that she continued serving the Lord and attended an Assembly of God Church nearby.

I trust God has given you a burden for souls, and you are praying for the salvation of the lost. However, also be ready for the Lord to use YOU to personally win them to Him! You want to experience that joy, don't you? If you don't feel a burden for souls yet, pray and ask God to give you that burden! "Ask, and you will receive, that your joy may be full" (John 16:24). God delights to answer that prayer. He's always looking for willing soul-winners!

Important Observations

First, God needed to give me a sign, in my case a literal sign (a real estate sign), to guide me to a church, a place where I would lead souls to Christ. The Lord is just as ready to give you signs and signposts to lead you into a fruitful place of personal evangelism. This book is but one signpost that was put in your hands in print or electronic form. I pray you will be convinced and learn how the Lord really can use anyone who desires to win souls to Him.

Second, Jack Hayford taught me how to witness effectively. I taught my youth group the same exact method, and some of them became personal evangelists. I showed Bob Brazell, by example, one method of evangelism. He repeated the pattern. I took the time to sit down with Grant Hollist and open the Scriptures to him. As a result of getting saved, he felt a deep hunger to attend Bible College to study the Bible more. This person-to-person-to-person method is God-ordained and is a biblical way to raise up an army of evangelists.

Third, leading a soul to Christ is pure joy. This alone should motivate us to gladly bear the cross of soul-winning. For many people, talking to others about Christ is one of the most difficult crosses! Like Christ, we must "despise (disdain) the shame" we might feel when witnessing. Crucify that shame because of the joy that will result! Follow…

"Jesus, the author and finisher of our faith, who for the joy that was set before Him endured the cross, despising the shame" (Hebrews 12:2).

Paul wrote,

"You have heard me teach things that have been confirmed by many **reliable witnesses**. Now teach these truths to other **trustworthy** people who will be able to **pass them on to others**" (2 Timothy 2:2 NLT).

Are you "a reliable witness?"

Are you "trustworthy?"

Will you "Pass these truths on to others?"

8

GIRLS, GIRLS, GIRLS... AND MY LAST GIRL, KATHY

"He who finds a wife finds a good thing and obtains favor from the Lord" (Proverbs 18:22).

If ever God created a man who needed a wife, I am that man! I seemed to have known this instinctively very early on. I kissed my first girl in kindergarten. Her name was Kathy. Must have been prophetic; that's my wife's name! Then, I went on my first date in the second grade. My mother took Kay Schnackenburg and me to the Los Angeles County Fair. Another time, I walked over to the home of Sandra Campa, one of the cutest girls at Cypress Elementary School. I hoped she

Sandy Campa. But no kiss, even with the honey!

would let me kiss her that day. Thus, I actually rubbed some honey on my lips, so in case she let me kiss her, my kisses would be SWEET! We didn't kiss that day, sadly, but oh, those bees!

In the 5th-grade, identical twin girls, Darlene and Charlene Wyborne, enrolled in our school. My buddy, James Fugate, went steady with Charlene, and I went steady for my first time with Darlene. She wore my ring on a chain around her neck. Back in the 1950s, that's what kids in grammar school did when a girl committed to one boy! Of course, within a week or two, they would likely be wearing some other guy's ring to show their now enduring commitment to him instead.

From kindergarten into 5th grade, I was in love with Barbara Warner. We shared most of the same classes until the 5th grade. My very first best friend, Kenny Johnstone lived across the street from me. We often sat in his front yard, and sometimes as I closed my eyes, he told a dreamy story about us driving up in our battery operated "Johnny Jeeps" to visit Barbara. Then he closed his eyes while I invented a similar love story. I tried and tried but just couldn't, for some reason, win Barbara's heart.

Somehow, I succeeded in the 5th grade! I can still easily envision the night our class went Christmas caroling. Barbara's dad owned a big truck he used to haul cattle. It had high sides in the back, maybe 3-to-4-feet high. Our class piled in the truck and rode around caroling. I can still see our teacher, Carl Pence, looking down at Barbara with me at her side and my arm around her for the first time in six years! Like all my early romances, it lasted only a few days or weeks.

In high school, I met a girl at a dance, and as usual, fell for her. At night, I knelt at my bed and prayed, "Oh Lord, please let this be the girl I grow up and marry!" It never entered my mind that she might also be on her knees at that very moment, praying, 'Oh Lord, when I grow up, please don't make me marry that Dea guy I met tonight!"-- canceling out each other's prayers, like at a football game with 50,000 praying one way and 50,000 others praying the opposite!

As described in Chapter 5, after Mary broke up with me, I continued in earnest pursuit of my future bride. I dated girls in the Bible College, but none of those worked out. So, I tried what's called "missionary dating" going out with unsaved sinner girls whose only qualification was that they were cute. My intent was to lead them to Christ, so I could then...well, it didn't work out that way. Christians, who marry someone unsaved, trusting that they could eventually lead them to Christ, often attest to their mistake. Many older women have stepped into my prayer line to ask me to pray for their husband, of many years, who was home watching TV instead of serving the Lord together with her! Singles, you've been warned!

Paul writes, "Do not be unequally yoked together with unbelievers" (2 Corinthians 8:14).

By my senior year at LIFE, I became highly discouraged because many of my classmates were either already married or engaged. I had all but given up on dating. What should I do? I counseled with a godly woman at college early in my senior year, telling her of my concern. She read to me a promise from the Word, "No good thing will He withhold, from those who walk uprightly" (Psalm 84:11). I began laying claim to that verse and asking God to bring me my "good thing."

During this very season, a girl in our Youth Group, Pam Horvath, carried a burden for one of her unsaved girlfriends, Kathy Basham. Pam was previously involved in a community church in Alta Loma, where Kathy attended. Sensing Kathy's need to be saved, Pam invited her, and invited her, and INVITED her to visit our church. Kathy later reports that the only reason she gave in to Pam was to "get her off my back."

Kathy and I at a Bible College awards banquet.

Just a few weeks after starting to pray the promise in Psalm 84:11, on October 12, 1969, I came to church as usual for a Sunday morning service. My habit was to walk into the sanctuary and greet the people already seated, especially the teenagers. As I walked in, I noticed some beautiful, auburn, long hair that I didn't recognize. I walked up to meet her and introduced myself. I discovered that the front view was even more beautiful! It was virtually love at first sight for me and Kathy became my last love! And it was only the 47th time in 20 years that I had fallen in love!

Pam Horvath drove Kathy home after the service. All afternoon Kathy was under conviction for her sin. That evening she came back to the church where at 9:05 PM, after our pastor's sermon, Kathy prayed at the altar getting right with God. I offered to drive her home after the service.

Before she left the car, I gave her our first kiss. Hey, don't be so judgmental! I had already known her for 10 whole hours!

I DON'T MESS AROUND, BOY!

Kathy Basham became the last girl I ever kissed romantically for over half a century!

Kathy, raised in a nominally Christian family, had some basic knowledge of Christianity as most other Americans do. She attended church. She sometimes would sit in the Orange Grove across the street from her home, meditating and trying to understand what her life was all about.

During her junior year of high school, God began to reveal His plan to this future woman of God.

One time while at her community church, before a service, Kathy noticed a poster advertising an evangelist coming to town. She didn't even know what an evangelist was and had to ask somebody.

As Kathy looked at the poster, the Lord spoke to her heart and said,

"One day you will be married to a man like that."

And I often remind her,

"AND WHAT A MAN!"

Immediately after we met, we began dating regularly and writing to each other.

I served as the editor of the college newsletter for a year. After receiving one of the letters Kathy wrote to me, I had the bright idea of sending her letter back to her, fully edited, in proper editor's style, marking all of her grammar, spelling, and punctuation errors.

She NEVER again wrote me another letter, even to this day!

We at least do phone calls and texts now…

"What a man!" indeed.

After picking Kathy up for our church's Christmas Eve candlelight service, I parked for a moment in a "romantic" industrial parking lot and proposed to her. She said, "Yes!" (What woman wouldn't have!). I placed a $75.00 engagement ring on her finger. Six months later, on June 25, 1971, we were married with Pastor Jack Hayford performing the

Leaving the ceremony for our honeymoon.

ceremony. That day happened to also be his birthday, again a sign of Jack's destiny in my life.

In those days, weddings were rarely the lavish affairs with catered dinners as most are now. The church where we married cost $75.00 to rent. The cake was home-baked and decorated by my Aunt Bobbie. My tuxedo was a used black Jacket I bought at a Goodwill store for $5.00. Fortunately, Kathy did not interpret all this as presaging a lifetime of marital poverty!

A highlight of the ceremony occurred when I sang to Kathy, though more slowly and romantically, Stevie Wonder's, "For Once in my Life." Decades later, Jack Hayford told me that the moment when I sang that song to Kathy was, "One of my most poignant memories." I only wish videotaped weddings existed back then. I could have submitted the recording of my song to America's Got Talent and probably won, with the golden buzzer!

Kathy and I honeymooned up the coast visiting San Francisco, at that time considered among the most beautiful cities in America. We then established our first residence in Crescent City in Northern California, where I had taken the position of Youth Minister for the Foursquare Church.

How and why Kathy and my first ministry ended up in Crescent City instead of just staying at Upland as Youth Ministers is an integral part of my life story. Let's go back a year in time...

In June of 1970, I graduated from Bible College and as a licensed minister, I was appointed as Youth Minister, instead of just Youth Leader, at the Upland Church. Yet, I still struggled in my spiritual life. From time to time, for instance, I would still sneak off to see a movie. In our orientation class at LIFE, Jack Hayford explained to the freshman why we had to sign an agreement to not attend movies. Basically, he used the

My LIFE Bible College graduation picture.

teachings in 1 Corinthians 8 and Romans 14 about not offending people.

Vivian Twyford, the Upland pastor, was older and had never been married. In fact, she attended LIFE while Aimee Semple McPherson still pastored there and served as President of the Bible College. Aimee founded the Foursquare church and is considered one of the most influential ministers during the first half of the 20th century. Sister Aimee created the "Crusader Covenant" for all teenagers who joined Foursquare youth groups to sign. Part of that covenant included a promise to never foray into such forbidden territories of the devil as, bowling alleys, dances, skating rinks or movie theaters. So, you can be sure that Pastor Twyford was against theaters!

I still struggled with legalism and sometimes even rebellion. So, I would "backslide" for a night, as in the good old days, and go see a movie. I would usually go far away, like seedy downtown Los Angeles, where I would be less apt to be seen. While buying my ticket at the box office, I'd cup my hand over my mouth a little to help disguise myself. Then, I'd slither down the aisle into a seat and slide as deeply as I could, hiding within the cushion.

After furtively glancing about just to make sure I, by some terrible coincidence, wouldn't be "discovered" by someone there who might know me, I'd finally try to enjoy the show. As the movie ended, I would quickly exit the building before they turned the lights back on, exposing the guilty hypocrite preacher!

My former college roommate, David Palmer, moved to Ontario and also ended up on the staff at Upland Foursquare as an assisting minister.

One night, I sat with David in his car admitting to him some of my struggles. I confessed that sometimes I even attended movies. I thought we were speaking in confidence, but I soon discovered otherwise. David reported to Pastor Twyford to, "Pray for Dea! He admitted to me that sometimes he goes to the movies."

Pastor Twyford's response needs a little background. Years previously, when she was pastoring another church, a man in her church was a homosexual. Apparently, he went to movies to meet other men. When David told her about me going to theaters, she quickly responded,

"Oh, I bet Dea is going there to meet other men!"

David lived with me, sleeping on the same bunk bed with me for a year. If anybody knew if I were a homosexual, it would surely have been him. David told her, "Oh no, Sister Twyford, I'm sure he's not doing that." But she had made up her mind and lamented, "Poor Kathy!" since we were already engaged to soon be married.

The next Sunday night, Sister Twyford preached on "Sodom and Gomorrah." I sat near the front enjoying her message. After she finished, I walked up to her and said, "That was a good sermon." I can still visualize her face, eyes closed, not wanting to look at me, her face in a slight grimace while she just nodded.

David realized that the Pastor directed her sermon towards me and that I was in the dark about it all. He called me and was very apologetic. He said, "Oh, Dea, I'm so sorry. I told Sister Twyford to pray for you because you were going to the movies." Then he explained that she now thought I was a homosexual.

It didn't end there. At the next district meeting for ministers, after the District Supervisor gave us a message, he called ministers forward who might need prayer. I got into the prayer line - always then, and always now, needing prayer. When I stood before him, without me saying a thing, he said to the others nearby, helping pray, "He has a personal problem." Pastor Twyford obviously had called the district office to give the evil report concerning me. The handwriting was on the wall.

I know God allowed this for His own purposes in my life. I loved being the Minister of Youth in that church. I loved my youth group. I carried no desire or plan to ever leave that ministry. The Lord, knowing that, had another idea for my life. He wanted to move me on to other training grounds and other ministries.

Just as the mother eagle kicks the eaglet out of the nest when the time comes for it to learn to fly, the Lord kicked me out of my comfortable nest. I decided that I would "fly" and do the work of an evangelist. I resigned from my position at the Upland Church.

I composed a letter of introduction, offering to come to speak in churches in California. Some pastors accepted my offer, and I ended up doing revivals in seven churches.

Souls were saved, and I had some of my very first experiences as an Evangelist. I also contracted the...

"sawdust trail fever."

The publicity photo I mailed out to introduce my ministry as an evangelist, in the typical pose of a sawdust trail preacher!

Nevertheless, God knew his evangelist was nowhere near ready emotionally or spiritually to be unleashed on the planet yet. Youth ministry remained a good fit for me at 22 years of age.

Still, I tried! I had mailed one of my evangelist introductory letters to the Crescent City Church. The youth minister had recently resigned, and Pastor Charles Randolph offered me the position. With only weeks remaining before my approaching wedding, the pastors of a church in El Cajon, where I recently held meetings, also offered me the position of Youth Minister at their church, confronting me with another life-changing decision.

I had to take into account my soon-to-be wife's welfare and not just my own. One evening, Kathy and I parked at one of my favorite all-time outdoor prayer closets, under eucalyptus trees on a dirt road at a farm not far from my parent's home. That evening was the very first of many, many times that Kathy and I would pray together, seeking to determine the will of the Lord in our decisions. After Pastor Randolph paid to have me fly up to meet him and see the church, it seemed like the best open door of the two. So, Kathy and I accepted our first ministry appointment together. We became the Youth Ministers in Crescent City, CA.

July 1971 to June 1972 became another very fruitful year in my life. The Charismatic and Jesus Movements were in full swing. As a result, many youths at the church were already on fire for God. That summer, something was happening six nights a week for the youth. Men, women, boys, and girls came to Christ because of the mighty move of God. I trained the youth in soul-winning techniques as I had my previous youth group. I led souls to Christ, and then, they led souls to Christ. Youth came to the altar seeking God regularly. Hippies and teenagers by the millions came to Christ all over America!

How I long to see such things again! I believe we will, which is one reason that I wrote this book!

My memories of working with youth in my first five or so years of ministry are precious. The joys of witnessing and the changed and transformed lives which I observed and became involved with made my writing this book all the more urgent. I believe another move of God among the youth of our nation is soon to take place.

Prepare for what's ahead!

- The Jesus movement focused our attention on Jesus.

- The Charismatic Movement focused our attention on the Holy Spirit.

- I believe that the next movement of God will especially focus our young people's attention on the Father!

Because of high divorce rates, single-parent households, and the media's mind-controlling influence on today's youth, they desperately need help. So many are without strong father images to guide and stabilize their lives. Thus, the Father Himself is going to visit America's youth to become THEIR FATHER.

Our witness, like John the Baptist's, will soon help to "turn the hearts of the fathers to the children, And the hearts of the children to their fathers, Lest I come and strike the earth with a curse" (Malachi 3:6). Surely the curse of homosexuality, transsexualism, abortion, drugs, and suicide among our youth is a clarion call for last day youth evangelists to do everything we can to stop any further progress of this curse! Lost souls wait for you to become a father-in-the-faith or mother-in-the-faith to them and to introduce them to their personal Savior and their Heavenly Father.

Have you found your "good thing" yet?

If you are single, you can trust the Lord to bring your helpmate in His time. Kathy was just in the 8th grade when I was a freshman in Bible College. Wouldn't I have looked silly bringing a junior higher to school activities! I wish I understood this truth before I roamed the highways and hedges of Southern California since kindergarten trying to find my wife!

Think about it! After two decades of searching, only weeks after I finally had decided to trust the Lord and stood on His promise, He supernaturally brought Kathy to me! Our son is now in his thirties and a LIFE Bible college graduate, yet he doesn't even date. Though he wants a wife, he truly is trusting God to bring her to him in His own time. I often give the following three verses to people who want me to pray with them to find their mate:

- "No good thing will He withhold from those who walk uprightly" (Psalm 84:11). You are walking uprightly, aren't you? Then you have a promise from God that He will not keep you from anything that is a "good thing" for you.

- "He that finds a wife finds a good thing" (Proverbs 18:22). So, men, a wife will be a "good thing" for you. And women, you will be a "good thing" for a man. Believe that marriage will be good for both of you!

- "Seek and you shall find...how much more will your Father who is in heaven give good things to those who ask Him" (Matthew 7:7, 11). Seek your mate in faith, your "good thing." You can go to singles groups, and you can go to Christian websites, but ultimately you should go to your Father in prayer. Don't be impatient! The word "seek" implies a period of time, so wait expectantly, but patiently.

Another Lesson: Trust the Lord also to lead and guide you to the college, the church, the Christian friends, the jobs, the city, to anything and anybody who will help you fulfill your calling in life. Moreover, always keep in mind that a big part of that calling will be to sometimes do the work of an evangelist.

Remember, you also may have to go through a difficult experience, as I did when I was accused of homosexuality. Nevertheless, when God leads you through a difficult valley, let me assure you after many years of observing His grace in my life, even the difficulties will work together for your good (Romans 8:28). Just as importantly, it will work for the good of lost souls who will escape hell because you are following the Lord's guidance in your life day-by-day.

Always trust that Jesus is paving the way before you. He "opens and no one shuts, and shuts and no one opens" (Revelation 3:7). In the next chapter, I will share many of those doors of service that the Lord opened for me. Stand in amazement with me at His ability to set the stage for you to personally lead someone to Him.

One final note in this pivotal chapter. A professional editor advised me to not include my wife's picture on the back cover because "the writer's picture only should be on the cover." Let me tell you a secret about my wife, Kathy. She is the "editor" that the Lord put in my life (Edit = to rearrange, to correct, to censor, to revise, to polish, and to fine-tune). She has done all those things with a similar passion to my passion for lost souls.

This book WOULD NOT HAVE BEEN WRITTEN without Kathy's wisdom as an abiding life-resource to me. Though Kathy prefers to sit at the back of a church while I preach, or stand silently by when I am witnessing, she is an editor and director behind the scenes of this book, "EVANGELIST".

On the front cover, you see Kathy holding my hand in our younger days, and she is still holding my hand on this journey today. I thus honor the hand-picked woman that God added to my life by adding her picture at my side on the first and last page of this book. May the last page of your life story which is even now being "written in the books" (Revelation 20:12) also testify that a husband and a wife can in truth be....

"Heirs together of the grace of life" (1 Peter 3:7).

Our two children, Nathan, and Carissa, in early childhood.

Just look at that hair! That face! That smile!
And then, look at Kathy's also!

9

SOUL-WINNING ADVENTURES

"Then Jesus said to them, "So wherever you go in the world, tell everyone the Good News" (Mark 16:15).

Where do I start? I recall so many memorable experiences leading souls to Christ. Instead of sharing them chronologically, I am dividing them up by categories over these next few chapters. Since each individual has his or her own strengths and weaknesses, I'll share the many varied methods of evangelism that I have used over the years. I trust as you read at least one of these stories, you'll tell yourself, "Hey! I can do that!"

Following are some of the more thrilling stories from my journey ...

Friends & acquaintances..."Return to your own house, and tell what great things God has done for you.' And he went his way and proclaimed throughout the whole city what great things Jesus had done for Him" (Luke 8:39).

After coming down from the mountain when I received Christ at Camp Cedar Crest, I soon started looking up old friends so I could witness to them.

I walked across the street to see my neighbor and friend, Kenny Johnstone. We had been friends since age four. I had no training yet but did the best I could talking about sin and hell and whatever else I could think of. Eventually, he closed the subject by saying, "I'm just not that bad." Kenny was the first person to whom I ever witnessed. I'll add more to Kenny's story later.

Norm Rush, 12th grade picture.

Then, I visited with my high school buddy, Norm Rush. As I shared with him, he came under conviction and wanted to know what he should do. I hadn't yet learned how to actually lead someone to the Lord, so we drove over to the Ontario Foursquare Church. Looking around, we found a LIFE upperclassman, who happened to be there. We sat down with her in the sanctuary. She clearly explained the gospel, probably using the same skills I would be learning within weeks in the Personal Evangelism class at LIFE. Norm gladly gave his heart to the Lord.

A few years later, he attended the Upland Foursquare Church, where I was the youth leader and where he met his future wife, Sue. Decades later, he continues serving the Lord as a faithful church member and even an adult Sunday School Teacher. We still stay in contact today and get together from time to time.

Since I graduated from high school a year early, almost all the youth my age were now seniors. I returned to witness on the Chaffey High School campus after school. Also, a church I attended with my sister when

I was little let this teenage preacher speak for an evening service. Hoping to win some of my friends to the Lord, I made hand-written invitations to the meetings. Then, during Chaffey's Friday night football game, I walked around passing the invitations out to old friends. Some came, probably just out of curiosity. I don't remember anyone getting saved, but planting seeds is important as well. That was, as I recall, my first church "evangelistic crusade" of hundreds more to come.

Neighbors ... "And who is my neighbor?" (Luke 10:29).

Witnessing to neighbors provides a unique class of evangelism. For one thing, you may only have one shot to shout the gospel across the fence, and if it doesn't work, well.... You likely have months or even years to bide your time for the most ideal moment to pull in the fish line! I have experienced the joy of winning some of my neighbors to the Lord.

A middle-aged woman lived across the street from a church where I pastored in Hawaiian Gardens, California. We exchanged small talk and neighborhood news from time to time when we happened to be outdoors and saw each other. The day finally came when I shared the gospel with her. She chose to give her heart to Christ. It was wonderful at last seeing her in church.

Our young family moved to Victorville, California in San Bernardino County about 80 miles northeast of Los Angeles where we lived for eight years while I evangelized the nation. An older man and his wife lived across the street. We visited briefly outside from time to time, as neighbors usually do. But after his wife died of cancer, I knew I had to do much more. So, I sat with him on lawn chairs in front of his house and we visited at length. He was a Catholic, but like many other Catholics, he hadn't been born again. I shared the truth with him, and he received the Lord.

When I pastored a church in Walla Walla, Washington, a couple lived downstairs from our apartment. We briefly talked from time to time, though I don't recall them ever coming to the services. After we moved to a house, I couldn't get them off my mind, so Kathy and I invited them over for dinner. After a good meal and a pleasant conversation, I earned the right to share the gospel with them. Both of them accepted Christ.

Pray for your neighbors regularly! Let your light shine before them. Invite them to church often. Prayerfully expect and be watching for that rewarding occasion when the Lord will provide a timely and proper venue to at last bare your soul to them.

Consider these suggestions

1. Invite neighbors over for coffee or a meal. Get to know them and their spiritual needs better if you haven't done this already.

2. When you see neighbors outside their home, in the yard, or driveway, hand them a good Christian book and say, "I read this book and it was really interesting. I think you'll enjoy it. Take a look and let me know what you think." Then, pray and see what door that book might open later.

Jesus was asked, "And who is my neighbor?" He answered with the story of the good Samaritan, "But a certain Samaritan, as he journeyed, came where he was. And when he saw him, he had compassion. So, he went to *him* and bandaged his wounds...and he set him on his own animal, brought him to an inn, and took care of him" (Luke 10:29-34). Have you "had compassion" on your "wounded" (by sin) neighbor? "Set him" in your own "animal" (Honda) and brought him to "an inn" (a church), to take "care of him." Ask yourself and the Lord, "And who is my neighbor?" Expect God to give you a burden and a strategy of how to best "take care" of his soul.

Invitations to church events…. "I was glad when they said to me, Let us go into the house of the Lord" (Psalm 122:1).

Recall from earlier in this book that my cousin invited me to a Christian Camp where I was saved. A girl in my youth group invited Kathy to our church, and she got saved. Most of you reading this probably came to the Lord because somebody asked you to one type of church event or another. I believe every Christian should invite, even COMPEL, people to church or church-related events on a regular, ongoing basis. My counsel is this: invite them, and invite them, and invite them again until they let you know, in no uncertain terms, that they are NOT interested, period! Until that point, with a smile on your face, just keep inviting them! You never know when they might say, "Yes!"

I've knocked on many, many doors over these past fifty years, inviting people to come to church or come to Christ. I've left many invitations to services and/or tracts at the door. Most who said they would come didn't, and that was always disappointing. But when those you invite finally come, it is so fulfilling.

For a period of time, I pastored a church in Hawaiian Gardens, a suburb of Los Angeles. One night, we scheduled a faith-based movie at our church for an evangelistic outreach. After printing up flyers, I went house-to-house for days, putting those invitations on thousands of doors, and thousands is not an exaggeration! While distributing flyers, I ran into a young lady on the sidewalk and handed her an invitation. She came that night and got saved. Others came too, but she was that only one who became a member of the church. A thousand invitations are not a waste of time even if only one accepts the invitation to come to Christ.

You might be thinking as you read this, "But, thousands of attempts with only one conversion!? That sure doesn't seem like a good return on the investment to me!" Well, tell that to a Mormon missionary. Estimates show that it takes 1,000 man-hours for those missionaries to gain one new member for their church!

Give a thousand invitations to church. Hand out a thousand flyers. Give out a thousand gospel tracts. Then, when only one soul escapes the fires of eternal hell, you can complain to the Lord about it when He comes. However, I promise you, that one soul won't be complaining! Plus, you never know who will respond. The work of an evangelist is to share the gospel and leave the results to God.

Another time, I was holding a crusade in a small Foursquare Church in Cheyenne, Wyoming. Every morning, I walked over to the nearby convenience store for a cup of coffee. A young woman worked the morning shifts. I started witnessing to her at the register and invited her to the meetings. Whenever someone walked in, I stepped away and stared at the candy rack. When they left, I started witnessing to her again. Someone else would walk in, and I'd step over to stare at the potato chip rack. Once they left, I'd go back to our witnessing conversation.

That revival was scheduled Sunday through Wednesday. Each morning I returned for my cup of coffee and witnessed to her once more. Again, and again, I invited her to the revival. Finally, it was Wednesday. That morning, I all but begged her to come to the final service saying, "This will be your last opportunity to come. Please come!" I handed her the flyer with the time and location of the service. That night, can you imagine my joy as I sat on the platform and saw her enter the back door coming into the service. When I finished preaching and gave the altar call, she came forward, joining a few others, to give her life to Christ.

Do the math! One invitation; no salvation. Two invitations, no salvation. Three invitations; no salvation. Four invitations; ONE salvation! It isn't rocket science. This formula has proven true across the centuries in the lives of millions of Christians; Christians like you, motivated by love, who never give up in their determination to compel the lost to come to Christ and to compel them to come to Church.

Visitation.... "I was sick and you visited me" (Matthew 25:36).

Visiting people where they live or their hospital room, their prison cell, or their rest home, provides a scriptural and proven effective means of evangelism.

While serving as the youth leader at Upland Foursquare, I made it my aim to visit the home of every teenager who attended our church. One evening, I went to see about the spiritual welfare of a teenage girl who had been to a service. Her teenage brother Gary was home, and I shared the gospel with them both. I don't remember her response, but Gary accepted Christ that day.

Later, Gary told me that initially, he responded just to end the conversation, but over time he realized that something happened in his heart. Gary came to church and became a vibrant member of the youth group. He later went on to graduate from LIFE, met and married a girl from the college, and eventually became a principal of a small Christian School in Oregon. I am so glad I bothered Gary that evening! Do you know anybody you could bother?

During my first pastorate in Sheridan, Wyoming, some elementary school-age girls visited our Sunday School. Their teacher gave me their address, and I called on the family that week. I led both of their parents to Christ, they started coming to the church, and the mother became our church treasurer!

Pastor, think seriously about either you or someone in your church visiting every visitor whom the Lord might send your way.

It can be a wide-open door when visiting someone with whom you have even a small connection and a valid reason to knock on their door. You can call ahead and make arrangements to come at a convenient time for them since in today's society, most people prefer advanced warning. But if and when you get into their home, this can become a nearly ideal atmosphere for a witnessing opportunity. Visiting a neighbor is proof of our fulfillment of Jesus' words "Love your neighbor as yourself" (Matthew 19:19)

Hospitals, especially, are excellent places to witness to a neighbor...

My Aunt Bobbie.

My Aunt Bobbie was in the hospital to have surgery. She previously showed no interest in spiritual things. But hospitals can be scary places! As she awaited her scheduled time to go under the anesthesia, I visited her room and talked with her about her soul. Thinking she might awaken from her surgery to the face of St. Peter, she listened carefully and prayed the sinner's prayer with me.

As I started to leave the room, the woman in the next bed, who obviously had overheard our conversation, said to me, "Oh, that was beautiful!" Well, that was like saying "Sick 'em to Lassie," so I stepped over to her bedside. She too prayed the sinner's prayer. I asked for her address and she happily gave it to me. That same week, I drove to her home, knocked on her door, and she invited me in. The woman, some of her in-laws, and her children all sat in the living room as I had the joy of sharing the gospel truth and then leading them all in praying the sinner's prayer.

To be a soul-winner, you must at times inconvenience people.

However, whatever inconvenience it may be for you or for them, it certainly won't be as inconvenient as hell, will it? They'll thank you when you run into them one day on the streets of gold!

One summer, as a college Christian Service assignment, I visited a rest home on Sunday afternoons. I walked into one room and met a 92-year old man resting in his bed. We talked and he explained to me that he managed a liquor store before he retired. He didn't know the Lord. I shared the glorious gospel with him and led him in the sinner's prayer. As I talked to him about salvation and heaven, I asked him, "Isn't that wonderful?" To which he, now cheerfully, replied, "Yes!"

The next weekend, I was excited to revisit my new convert but when I arrived, I discovered his room was empty. I inquired, and the nurse told me that he died just two days after I saw him last. Just think! The Lord allowed that man to live years beyond the average life expectancy of men. Why? Because He knew that someone would do the work of an evangelist and take time to visit him, just in the nick of time to save his soul.

Elderly people sit in their wheelchairs or bedridden in assisted living centers or even their own homes. Many have no family or friends who take time to visit them. Most of them are absolutely thrilled to have someone visit. Think about leaving your TV football game next Sunday afternoon to be a bearer of good news to someone, someone who may the following week enter eternity.

Note: hospitals and rest homes are stricter now about who can visit patients. Try sneaking a quick look at the patient registry, notice a name, say John Smith, and tell the nurse or receptionist that you want to visit John Smith. Then visit him, and afterward go from room to room like you own the place! You could also plan some visits through your church connections. I promise you will never experience so many welcome arms! I have been "kicked" out of more than one place, but witnessed while I could!

Automobiles... "Then the Spirit said to Philip, "Go and enter that chariot" - or Chevy! (Acts 8:29).

The privacy of a vehicle provides a near-perfect environment for a presentation of the gospel. When a hitchhiker has been invited into your automobile and you are helping him, for free, you have earned the right to talk and say whatever you want. Similarly, if you are paying an UBER driver to take you somewhere, I have discovered that, almost without exception, he or she will listen to your witness.

Hitchhiking isn't as common, or as safe, these days, but when I was in Bible College, hitchhikers were ubiquitous. I picked up a teenager on my way to church one Sunday morning. After giving him the gospel, he prayed the sinner's prayer with me. He was but one of many strangers I'd led to the Lord, yet I had no way of knowing if most of them really had a life-transforming experience, I began feeling discouragement. Is this really worth all this effort?

Then, weeks later, on my way to church, that teenager I picked up previously was again hitchhiking. I gladly picked him up. When I asked him if he could tell any change in his life since he had accepted the Lord, he replied, "Yes. I seem to be happier." After letting him out, I drove away, thankful that the Lord gave me a confirmation. Here's a soul-winner's promise:

"Therefore, my beloved brethren, be steadfast, immovable, always abounding in the work of the Lord, knowing that your labor is not in vain in the Lord" (1 Corinthians 15:58).

I rarely pick up hitchhikers anymore. It can be very dangerous! My cousin, Thurmond Millhollen, who was a very godly man, once picked up a hitchhiker who pulled out a knife to rob him. Thurmond put his finger to his lips and said, "Shhh, everything we're saying is being recorded." The thief, panicky, cried, "Stop this car and let me out!" Wouldn't you like to have that presence of mind during a robbery!

A friend of mine told me about his brother, who was a strong witness for Christ. Seeing another opportunity to shine his light for Jesus, he picked up a hitchhiker. However, the strange man pulled out a gun, shot and killed him, and stole his car. When they arrested the murderer and asked him why he had committed such an egregious crime, he said, "I just wanted to get back in prison." Be sure you are led by the Spirit when you pick up a hitchhiker! By the way, that evil hitchhiker's last name was "Warford" (gulp!).

I have experienced the joy of leading UBER and LYFT drivers to the Lord. I often call them to take me to the airport to catch a flight.

As I conversed with one driver, he reported that he was a Catholic, but he didn't attend church. I carefully shared the gospel with him, and he accepted the Lord. I took the time to explain the importance of and urged him to find a good church, maybe an evangelical one instead of Catholic. As he let me out of the car, he reported, "I will find a church!" Lead them to Christ in automobiles and then help lead them to a good church!

I was picked up by a man from Uganda. He was my Uber driver when I was coming home from a meeting back east. I soon discovered that he was a Catholic. Witnessing to him, I carefully added the truth, "Jesus said we must be born again to enter the

Uber driver new convert.

kingdom." He asked, "How are you born again?" God was working! I fully explained the basics of the gospel and led him in the sinner's prayer. As I left the car, I gave him my card and told him to call me if I can help him. He said, "We could pray together?" A sign that he was deeply moved! You can deeply move people too!

At the Tucson, Arizona International Airport, I hailed a taxi. The driver turned out to also be a Catholic from Africa, but this time from Sudan. He'd never been born again with no assurance of salvation. After hearing the gospel, he gladly received Christ. I wish you could have seen him as he shook his fists in the air and prayed fervently as I led him in the words. As we parted ways, I assured him, "I'll see you in heaven." He shot back, "For sure!"

Help them to know for sure! Be on the lookout at all times for...

Spirit-led taxi or any other type of evangelism openings!

10

MORE ADVENTURES

"Come, follow me," Jesus said,
"and I will send you out to fish for people"
(Matthew 4:19 NIV).

Three-time World Heavyweight Boxing Champion Muhammed Ali is now dead. As a young disenchanted African American he was walking down the street one day. A man standing outside of a Muslim temple saw him, walked up to him, and invited him inside.

The Muslims called it "fishing".

Ali went into the building. On that tragic day, though raised in the Christian faith, Ali converted to Islam!

Oh, would to God that but one Christian in just one of the churches that Ali had walked by that day would have left their coffee in the foyer and stepped outside to "fish for men." Had they done so, and had Ali committed his life to Christ, that fisherman for the Lord would have caught the future "Sportsman of the 20th Century." Imagine the gospel impact that Muhammed Ali could have had as the sport's idol of his generation!

Jesus said, "…I will send you out to fish for people".

Will you allow Him to send you outside the four walls of your church?

Fish for people!

The streets are wide open for such fishing. We call this "street evangelism"…

Streets... "Then the master told his servant, 'Go to the roads and paths! Urge the people to come to my house. I want it to be full" (Luke 14:23 GW).

3 Basic Methods of Street Evangelism

1. You can stand on a corner and just start preaching away to anyone who might listen. I tried this form of street evangelism many years ago; although, most people would be very uncomfortable doing this.

    A pastor told me about a time that he and his congregation set up their music and loudspeakers and started preaching outdoors. A man across the way began shooting at them. They all stood their ground, willing to die for Jesus, though unhurt, yet frightened for their lives! The pastor told me, "I'll never do that again!"

2. You can stand on a corner with tracts in your hand, ready to speak to anyone willing to give you a moment. Jehovah's Witnesses do this, but I can't remember ever seeing anyone approach them or talk with them about their magazines. Personally, I don't have the patience to use this method but it might fit your personality well.

3. By far the most effective method is to approach strangers on the street, strike up a conversation, or ask them, "Have you read this yet?" while handing them a tract and allowing the discussion to unfold.

My most memorable street evangelism experience occurred while pastoring in Sheridan, Wyoming. One Saturday night, during a prayer meeting, I suddenly felt a strong burden to hit the streets to witness. One of the young men joined me and we drove downtown.

As I looked for someone to approach, a group of teenagers walked out of a pizza parlor. We approached them and I said, "Hey! Where are you headed?" One of them sheepishly pointed down the street. I said, "No, I mean when you die!"

With that, I began preaching the gospel to them. When I asked them to pray with me to accept Christ, most of them did so right on that sidewalk! One of them named Becky Moreland started attending the church, eventually served as a youth leader for a while, and even went to Bible College for a year. I lost track of her over time.

Decades later, Becky researched and found my present location. She phoned me, and we talked for maybe half-an-hour. Becky referred to me as, "My father in the faith." Over and over again, she told me, "I love you," to the point that I felt embarrassed.

I am so glad that I obeyed the promptings of the Holy Spirit and did a little street ministry. Keep open to the Lord, and He may soon have a job for you to do downtown.

There are other good venues for soul-winning adventures…

Stores… "Preach the word of God. Be prepared, whether the time is favorable or not. Patiently correct, rebuke, and encourage your people with good teaching" (2 Timothy 4:2 NLT).

Convenience store convert.

I went into a convenience store to get a diet coke. A man in line (Left) struck up a conversation with me. As I walked out of the store with Kevin, a middle-aged, heavyset man, I told him that I was an evangelist and handed him my tract. He said, "I try to do good things, and God helps me." I replied, "Yes, but the Bible says that no one will make it to heaven by good works. You have to be born again." He responded, "How are you born again?" Oh, I love to hear people ask me that question! As people walked past us coming in and out of the store, I gave him the gospel. He prayed the sinner's prayer along with me right there in the parking lot!

My glasses needed adjustment, so I visited an optician. The owner's wife

She felt CHILLS!

(left) was helping me. I started witnessing to her. She thought she would likely go to heaven because she was good. I asked her if she had ever lied. She said, "No." I asked her if she had ever stolen. She said, "No." Then I asked her if she had ever used God's name in vain. That was the right question because she admitted that very morning she had blasphemed, "because I got mad at my nephews." I then warned her by quoting the verse, "The Lord will not hold him guiltless who takes His name in vain" (Exodus 20:7).

Before long, convinced that she was a sinner in need of a Savior, she prayed the sinner's prayer with me. Afterward, she said, "I feel CHILLS!" Help someone feel the "chills" of salvation today!

Laundromats - or anywhere you find people standing, sitting, or waiting... "A man who has friends must himself be friendly" (Proverbs 18:24).

You can become the best friend any sinner ever had! But don't wait for him to come to you! Go to him! One evening, while pastoring in Lakeview, Oregon, I took a walk. As I passed by a laundromat, I noticed a woman and her young daughter doing their wash. They were the only ones in the building. This provided an ideal witnessing opportunity, but I just wasn't in the mood. Watching from the opposite side of the street, I struggled for a while; my spirit and soul in mortal combat over a soul-winning opportunity. The flesh has perfected this battle! Finally "a spirit of power and of love and a sound mind" (2 Timothy 1:7) triumphed over fear and I walked across the street to the laundromat.

After introducing myself, I started a conversation with the woman. She didn't attend church and didn't yet know the Lord. However, by the time I left, she had accepted the Lord and soon attended our church. Her husband came and also got saved too. Years later, I happened to run into him in a completely different city. Though the couple had divorced, and he had done some time in jail, he was still serving Christ!

Parks... "Jesus said, 'Make the people sit down.' Now there was much grass in the place. So, the men sat down" (John 6:10).

Parks with shade trees and soft grass provide a great place to sit and relax. Parks can also provide a great opportunity to evangelize! I live in an apartment at the Florence Avenue Foursquare Church in Santa Fe Springs, California. I'm a runner, and I hate treadmills so I enjoy running outdoors. I have my favorite routes, one of which includes running through a park about a mile from home. While jogging, I frequently saw a homeless man. I knew he was homeless because he had a shopping cart and there isn't a supermarket within miles! I kept seeing him, and he kept seeing me. One time, he told me his name was Jaime. As I ran by, I would say "hi" or give him a quick blessing or quote a verse from the Bible to him. Once I stopped long enough to hand him my tract. I inquired, and he pointed out to me the bushes in the park where he slept at night.

Finally, one Saturday, I told Jaime, "My church is right around the corner, and if you come to the service tomorrow at 9 AM, I'll take you out afterward for Mexican Food. With no speaking engagements scheduled that weekend, on Sunday morning I stood in front of the church watching for Jaime. Sure enough, he showed up across the street finishing a cigarette before heading toward the church.

I greeted Jaime, and his first concern was where he could put all the valuables he had been guarding with his life. I knew Pastor Terry Risser wouldn't want that stuff sitting in the foyer, so I helped him find a good place to hide it around back, where he'd feel secure about it while he was in the service, and where none of the church members would be tempted to steal his old sleeping bag or his designer wardrobe.

We sat together for the service, but Jaime didn't respond to the altar call that day. Afterward, I took him to the nearby Mexican restaurant and treated him, as I had promised. The entire experience provided a good time of witnessing too. Sitting, waiting, then enjoying a meal together is another great way to minister and win souls!

A few weeks later, when I wasn't on one of my usual out-of-town trips, I was tickled to see Jaime come to church again. We sat together, and when the pastor gave the altar call, I noticed him lift his hand. As Pastor Terry called people forward, I invited him to come up with me. He came forward and prayed the sinner's prayer. Then, I introduced him to the pastor.

Jaime and his cart have moved on for greener pastures. I haven't seen him for years. I don't know if he continued in the faith, but I do know that I did the work of an evangelist in a park, and I'm glad I did. Park yourself next to a sinner in a park soon.

Co-Workers..."Let some grain from the bundles fall purposely for her" (Ruth 2:15).

The Scripture above comes from the story of Ruth when Boaz instructed his hired hands to purposely provide grain for Ruth's needs. Likewise, at your workplace, purposely make your bundles and grains of truths available for your co-worker's needs.

In the 1970s, I took over a small church restart in Fruitland, Idaho. To supplement our income, I found a job building motor homes in a nearby factory. When we moved from Southern California, I brought my moped to ride to work. It soon broke down, so my lead man offered to pick me up and take me home, as it was on his way to work. As we commuted together, seeing my golden opportunity, I began witnessing to him. I explained the gospel fully and led him to Christ. That evening, I visited his home and also led his wife to Christ!

When the motorhome factory closed, I found a job as a radio advertising salesman. I parked downtown and entered one business and then the next, asking to speak to the owner or manager so we could discuss advertisement options. At a shoe store, the young woman inside said she was a salesgirl. We were the only ones in the store, so I took advantage of this opportunity and gave her the gospel. She knelt with me at the seats where people try on shoes. While I hoped and prayed nobody came in the store and interrupted that moment, I led her in the sinner's prayer.

The salesgirl had already informed me she was living with her boyfriend. I told her that now that she was a Christian she needed to tell him that she couldn't sleep with him anymore unless they were married. She must have followed my advice because I received a phone call that same night from her boyfriend. He told me that he wanted to talk to me. I invited him over to my office, and to be honest, I was scared that he was going to beat me up! The milk wasn't free anymore, as the old saying goes. Tragically, American youth today want everything to be free, including sex.

Was I relieved as we sat down in my office and talked! Actually, he wasn't upset, only curious about it all. I gave him the good news, and he prayed the sinner's prayer with me. To my pleasant surprise, afterward, he immediately, joyously cried, "Praise God!" He obviously encountered the Savior. They came to the church, but soon, thereafter, I resigned the pastorate and left them in God's hands. Evangelists catch the fish but often must let others clean and fry them!

During one Christmas season, I was still at my job selling radio advertising. The Friday afternoon before our Christmas Party, none of the workers at the radio station were in the mood to work, so we sat around visiting and waiting for the official quitting time of 5 pm. As we chatted about this and that, I sneakily turned the conversation over to spiritual things. As I told some of my experiences, one of the women said, "I just don't understand it all!" Seeing the open door, I said, "Come on downstairs to the restaurant, let's have a cup of coffee and talk." We did, and before long, while seated at our table drinking our coffee, with tears in her eyes, she received Christ.

That night, as my co-worker entered the home where the party was held, I greeted her at the door. She introduced her husband to me. As I shook his hand as he said, "So you're the guy she's been talking about!" We found a place to sit in the main room, with most people drinking alcoholic beverages. I didn't drink, and the new convert and her husband weren't drinking heavily. As the party got louder and wilder, I asked them if they would like to leave and join me at a nearby restaurant for a cup of coffee. They did.

As we visited in the restaurant, I explained the fundamental biblical truths to the husband that I had already shared with his wife. Eventually, I asked him if he would like to get right with God. At first, he hesitated and explained why. He had a job delivering beer and figured that he would have to quit that job to be a Christian. I assured him he did NOT have to do that and explained why. I knew by experience that if he really committed his life to Christ, it wouldn't be long before the Lord would help him get a more edifying job. Now relieved, he prayed the sinner's prayer with me over our coffee. Hey! I just got a revelation of the REAL reason God created coffee! Coffee drinkers, let this become your personal revelation too! Let's call it "Coffee and Christ!"

Gospel Tracts... "The Lord gives the word: great (is) the host of the publishers" (Psalm 68:11 DBY).

I began carrying tracts with me while still a freshman in Bible College, and I still carry them with me today. In fact, I even wrote and published my own tract called, "Where and When." I keep several folded in the iPhone case that I wear on my belt to carry my pocket New Testament. I hand tracts out from time-to-time: restaurants, taxi drivers, airplanes, etc. I've left many tracts with an enclosed buck or two as a tip in motels where I stay. I watch to see the nationality of the cleaning maids, and if they look Hispanic, I leave the Spanish version of my tract which I carry folded up in my wallet. Sometimes I also leave a note that says,

"I wrote this, please read it!"

I remind you again, a copy of my tract "Where and When" is included in the back of this book.

It's been my experience that a tract itself rarely results in a conversion. So, you might think, "Isn't it then a waste of your time to hand them out?" You decide after reading the following story.

Nearly two decades ago, I started a personal physical exercise regimen. I work out diligently because I read where a medical doctor said, "Physical exercise is the closest thing to a fountain of youth." My goal is to continue to preach the gospel as an evangelist into my eighties! Yet, even as I write this book, the angel of death is chasing me and he's getting closer and closer every day! Pray for me, that I can keep ahead of him!

I usually lift dumbbells in my office and jog around the neighborhood, as I am always trying to save time. But for some reason, I now know why I decided one afternoon to go to the nearby LA Fitness to work out. See the fruit of that guidance...

Father and son both accepted Christ.

At the gym, as I lifted dumbbells, a young man worked out next to me. Usually, men don't do much visiting while working out. Weightlifting is hard work! Besides, men like to just stare into the mirror and admire their growing muscles. However, this young man loved to talk. As we spoke in-between sets, he asked me what I did. I told him, "I am a writer." Then I gave him one of my tracts. I said, "Read it, my phone number is on the back if you would like to discuss it further."

That evening he called and said that both he and his father read the tract. He said, "We're both excited about it." I asked him if I could come over one evening so we could have a Bible study together. He was glad for me to do so. A few nights later, while seated in their living room, I shared with the two of them this glorious gospel. They had been raised Catholics but had never been born again. Before long, they both knelt at the coffee table. That evening, I led a father and his son to Christ.

Take a quick look at my tract at the back of this book, which you are welcome to copy and print all you want on your home printer with your name and phone number on it!

If you will take the time to do this, you can become a publisher for Jesus! By so doing, you can be one of those Psalm 68:11…

"host of the publishers."

Give the devil a headache now! Write your name in the blank below:

I, _____ am a publisher for Jesus!

Calling people to the altar of repentance in Lubbock, TX.

11

DOOR TO DOOR EVANGELISM

"I have taught you publicly, and from HOUSE TO HOUSE, testifying both to the Jews, and also to the Greeks, repentance toward God, and faith toward our Lord Jesus Christ" (Acts 20:20, 21).

I understand that not everybody has the extrovert personality to knock on the doors of strangers. However, I am an extrovert among extroverts, the first one to talk on elevators, and the one kicked out of classes in school for trying to be funny or disrupting the class! I am also a born salesman and started going out door-to-door selling things while still in grammar school. Full-time evangelists have a specific genetic code. Not everyone carries the evangelist's genes, but all can learn from them.

Once my father bought a bunch of peaches from a local farmer, and while he walked on one side of a street knocking on doors, I walked on the other doing the same. When my dad made a delivery at a home where I had sold a box, the man insisted that he step out in the back with him. The man pointed out a peach tree, full of the same variety of peaches I sold him and said...

"Here I have all these peaches and your son talked me into buying his peaches. If you don't make him a salesman!"

Office gift evangelists are usually born salesmen. They make good car salesmen, for example. Case in point, the first job I ever had as a car salesman, during the first two weeks, I sold more cars than all the other salesmen. Throughout the years, I have gone out by myself door to door selling, I should say, GIVING away the gospel quite a few times.

Norm Rush told me that when we were in high school, I was, "the bravest person I've ever known. You weren't afraid of anything!" That isn't true, and I have to fight lots of my own fears, but at least I am certainly not afraid to knock on doors for the Lord. When God calls a man or woman to be an evangelist, He gives them the inherent talents and strengths to fulfill that ministry.

I don't share the above to impress you. Rather, I share this to keep you from any sense of shame or inadequacy if you happen to feel that you just could not knock on doors. Some, like I, can and so I included this proven method of reaching the lost. Door-to-door is my favorite type of personal evangelism. After a knock and a few brief words, you know to either move on, or you discover a ready audience and another wonderful opportunity to share your faith. In today's world, it is safer, especially for women, to go in pairs just as Jesus sent his disciples into the world in pairs.

I was chased off a property by a man with a pitchfork, but that was only once. I know some of you are afraid of dogs. While holding a revival, I took a pastor with me door-to-door to witness and invite people to his church. I soon discovered that he was terribly fearful of dogs. So, if there was a dog in a yard, he stood outside the gate while I went up to the door and knocked. "Hi, I'm evangelist Dea Warford," and while pointing at the pastor a safe distance away, I'd say, "that is Pastor so and so."

Incidentally, at one time, I worked for the Humane Society and knocked on thousands of doors to check dog licenses. I discovered that if a dog barked or looked vicious, all I had to do was hold my hand over the fence. If he headed for my hand, I'd just pull it back; he bites! But if the dog just sat barking at my hand, he wasn't going to attack my torso! More than once someone answered the door after I walked right past their supposedly vicious dogs. They'd ask me, "How did you get in here? Those dogs don't let anybody in here!" I also learned that if the gate was closed, but no dog was visible, to shake or rattle the gate loudly and wait a moment. If there was an unchained dog in the back, he'd run out front immediately. Try it sometime!

Don't let dogs keep you from knocking on a door for Jesus! God has given those who carry the gospel a promise to claim over the animal world. "Go into all the world and preach the Good News to everyone. (Everyone includes those who live in houses, doesn't it?). "They will be able to handle snakes with safety" (Mark 16:15, 18 NLT). If we can "handle snakes with safety," then we can certainly handle a dog or two!

Some erroneously think door to door evangelism just isn't very fruitful. Tell that to the Mormons and Jehovah's Witnesses! Why should they have a corner on the market? Door to door evangelism can bear real fruit! Let me share some personal illustrations to prove my point.

One time, when I was holding a crusade in Burlington, Washington, I invited one of the men in the church to go door-to-door witnessing with me. The next day we knocked on doors until we came to a house where a teen answered the door. There were several others sitting in the living room, obviously just talking. I explained why we were there and asked if we might come in and talk awhile. They were willing. I'll let Pastor Don Counter tell you in his own words what happened...

"Dea and another brother in our church went out into the neighborhood and led 4 young people, ranging in ages from 17-19 to the Lord. These people were excited about Jesus, and in the next year, helped lead approximately 50 others to Christ. As a result of this ministry, I baptized 26 young people in 13 weeks."

Hmm, clearly it was worthwhile to go door-to-door that afternoon. What might you accomplish if you went out door to door?

Another time, while pastoring a church in Los Angeles County, I once took John Vallejo, a Bible College student from our church, door-to-door witnessing with me. We hadn't knocked on many doors when we came to a house where a woman invited us in. John observed attentively as I carefully explained the gospel to the woman. She was ready and received Jesus that very hour!

John later became a senior pastor, a missionary to South America, and is now a District Supervisor over the Foursquare Hispanic churches in the Southern California District. He later told me that I was the one who taught him how to lead souls to Christ.

Pastor, mature saint, "born salesmen," imagine showing, not just telling, some young person how to lead souls to Christ. Door-to-door evangelism certainly lends itself to that end, and also puts you in the same vein as Paul the Apostle who said, " I... have taught you publicly and from house to house" (Acts 20:20 NIV).

Door to door is truly, in my experience, one of the best soul-winning methods. Here are the reasons why.

- If people aren't home, you can still leave an evangelistic tool on their door and make a note of their address and come back again.

- If they are home, they are often just lounging around or watching TV. Some people enjoy the company or conversation. Others will stand at the door for quite a while talking and I have been invited in many times.

- They live in your community, and if they aren't going to church, you can get the first claim on them! Knock on enough doors and you will find someone who recently moved into the neighborhood or someone who is lonely, suicidal, or for manifold reasons is ready to listen to someone who might have answers. You DO have answers!

- You can quickly determine if they are interested or not so that you don't have to waste your time or theirs.

- Systematically, over the long-haul, your church can reach every house in your community.

I have tried many approaches through the years in door to door ministry. I have used the "We're taking a survey" avenue. I have even cut to the chase with, "Do you have a satisfying relationship with Jesus Christ?" When I pastored in Walla Walla, Washington I went door to door and asked that question. One young woman named Sherry admitted she did not. She was backslidden, but listened as I explained how she could "have a satisfying relationship with Jesus Christ." She returned to the Lord and started coming to our church where I further ministered to her.

I believe the door-to-door method I use and will explain below has the greatest potential for success. It is best to go out in groups of two. "The Lord now chose seventy-two other disciples and sent them ahead in pairs" (Luke 10:1 NLT). One woman and one man are ideal, especially in today's society!

Apartments and mobile home parks, I've found, are usually more productive areas to start than just tract homes. Less affluent and more transient people are less apt to be already established in a church. You can also knock on far more doors in less time. If the apartments or trailer parks have signs out front that say, "No Soliciting", just walk right past them and start knocking. You aren't soliciting. You are obeying the Great Commission! But DO NOT knock on the manager's door, or they will tell you to get out!

Begin by knocking on a door and with a big smile say, "Hi, my name is Adam and this is Eve. We are from the Assembly of God Church on 1st and Main, and we are just out inviting people to visit our church." That is, in my opinion, the least threatening approach at a door when you are a complete stranger. You have a flyer, tract, or church bulletin in your hand, not a big Bible or big black briefcase, or they might think you are one of those, you know who. Hold the flyer, tract, or bulletin out towards them as you talk.

If they refuse to open the door or say, "I'm not interested," just smile and say, "God bless you" and move on to the next door. There must be a reason why Jehovah's Witnesses will come back again and again to the same house, even though the occupant never has shown any interest. There has hardly been an hour or session going door to door that I haven't had at least one person open the door, take their free gift, allow me to continue the conversation, invite me in, or accept Christ.

I'll often ask, "Do you go to church anywhere REGULARLY?" (Very important adverb). Many feel that even just an occasional visit to church qualifies them as a believer. We know better. How they respond tells you volumes about their spiritual life. If they show evidence of being born again, but don't attend church regularly for one reason or another, encourage them to visit yours. If you don't like their answer and doubt that they are saved, then you can go as far as they are willing to let you go in explaining the gospel to them at their door. If I sense openness, I'll often ask, "May we come in and talk about it a little?" If they invite you in, you have basically been given carte blanche to share the gospel, graciously and humbly of course, as it is their home after all!

I recently received an email from a lawyer, Sunny Wise, who was a teenage girl at the time (1971). She reported, "You challenged my faith by making me walk with you door-to-door in Johannesburg, California to introduce you and invite people to our Church." Note her choice of words, "making me."

I used to have little empathy for people who weren't as bold as I was. Now I realize that this kind of ministry is not for everyone. And I truly do not want you to feel guilty if you are less dedicated than the Mormons and Jehovah's Witnesses... just kidding!

Repeat after me please, "Door to door"...

"Door to door"...

Say it, come on now, I know you can do it...

"Door to door is one effective means to evangelize my community."

There! Don't you feel better already? If door to door evangelism is something you know you could do, then call or email and discuss it today with your pastor. When you start out.... Don't forget to bring someone with you. Don't forget your pocket New Testament. Don't forget your tracts...

AND don't forget to wear that smile!

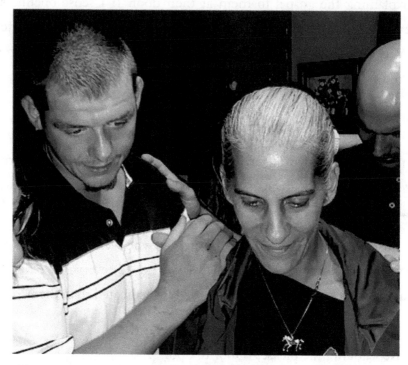

New converts, who accepted Christ after we took a team out
door to door in New York, receiving our prayers for them
after they joined us for a service.

12

A HIGH-FLYING EVANGELIST

"Philip ran over and heard him reading from the book of the prophet Isaiah. He asked him, 'Do you understand what you are reading?" The official replied, 'How can I understand unless someone explains it to me?' And he invited Philip to climb up and sit in the carriage with him" (Acts 8:30, 31 GNT).

As a traveling evangelist, I encounter unique occasions to witness as I am frequently seated next to someone on an airplane for hours at a time. Even if you don't fly very often, the examples of soul-winning shared in this chapter can be duplicated anytime you might encounter a relatively private listener for a long enough length of time. The golden-opportunities I have experienced resulted in a number of exciting conversions.

While waiting to board a jet in Midland, Texas, I sat in a terminal next to a man named Chris. As we visited briefly, I gave him my tract. He saw my phone number on the back and said he might call me because he'd like to talk further. I witnessed to him, but we soon heard our boarding call. I sat toward the rear of the plane and wondered if he would come back and sit by me. He didn't. After the plane leveled off at high altitude, I thought about how Jesus purposely sat by a well so that He could talk to a sinful woman (John 4).

I decided to be intentional and walked up to the front of the plane where Chris was seated. I told him, "I'm seated in the back with no one else in my row if you would like to join me and talk more." He followed me back to my seat. Chris then told me his story. He used to be an alcoholic, but five years ago Jesus appeared to Him. Soon after, he was delivered from alcohol. He prayed and tried to be a Christian ever since. Yet, he never joined a church, got baptized by immersion, or learned to study the Bible.

I had to take the initiative with this man!

I told Chris that the Lord appeared to him to show how much He loved him and to deliver him from alcohol. However, Chris still needed to repent of his sins and receive Christ into his life. We talked for some time about the things of God and the way of salvation. After explaining that he needed to be born again, he willingly prayed the sinner's prayer with me and committed his life to Christ. What if I hadn't taken the initiative to invite Chris, pictured above, to sit with me? Soul-winners must often seize the initiative when eternal souls are at stake!

Another time, on my way to speak in Kalamazoo, Michigan, I sat by a college student studying to be a doctor. During the flight, she took out some pills and swallowed one. Curious, thinking, maybe they were motion sickness pills, I asked her what they were. She said, "birth control pills." I was embarrassed that I could be so naïve! Thankfully, the Lord was able to use that faux pas later.

As we discussed her life, she said she was unmarried, yet had a boyfriend, whom she was obviously sleeping with (by taking birth control pills). I pointed out to her that the Bible says,

"The fornicator shall not inherit the kingdom of God" (1 Corinthians 6:9, 10).

After explaining what it meant to repent of sins and to be born again, she willingly prayed the sinner's prayer with me.

Birth control **pills** helped me present the **gos-pill**!

God will use your gaffes too! By keeping quiet, you'll never make any gaffes, but you will also never lead a soul to Christ!

Children need Jesus too!

I hesitate to preach to children when sitting next to one on a jet (for obvious reasons: an older man leaning toward them quietly talking!) Nevertheless, I dared to speak about the Lord to the boy pictured on the right. I asked him, "If you were to die today, what do you think are the percentage odds you would go to heaven?" He answered, "80%." I then asked him, "If the pilot announced that the odds of this jet crashing were 80%, would you have gotten

Kids need Christ too!

on it?" He said, "Maybe if I were 80 years old." (Young people today think we over 60 gang could care less if we die in a fiery plane crash or not.

We're already so miserable anyway!). Long story short, he prayed the sinner's prayer with me and I left him with some strong counsel for his future life!

Great sinners need Christ

Forgiven of two great sins!

A precious lady sat next to me on another plane. We engaged in small talk for a while, then we got down to business! She confessed that she was once a Catholic until she committed, in her words, "two great sins." She obviously felt very convicted about these sins so began attending a protestant church. Yet, she was not born again. I experienced the joy of praying with her to get saved.

Just look at that smile after she'd received Christ!

Families Need Christ

A father and son come to Christ.

On a jet flying into Dallas, Texas, I sat by a man and his seven-year-old son. I discovered that he was quite talkative. He and his son were flying to see a professional football game. We talked about sports and about his life. Then I brought up the subject of religion. Soul-winners can't wait for others to bring that subject up. You could talk with most people forever and they would never bring it up! He was a Catholic and admitted that he only went to church on special holidays. Yet, he felt he would probably go to heaven because "I don't hurt anybody and I am always honest." He admitted that, though unmarried, he was living with his girlfriend. With the help of THAT knowledge, it didn't take many Scriptures or very long to bring him under conviction for his sin and to a point of making a decision for Christ. After leading him in prayer, I turned to his son and asked, "Would you like to invite Jesus into your heart?" He smiled and answered, "Yes." This was the first time, to my recollection, that I had led both a parent and their child to the Lord on a jet.

On another Southwest Airlines flight, I sat by a woman (right). After gaining her trust through preliminary conversation, she admitted that her life was "spinning out of control and at the lowest point of my life." She was ripe and ready to hear the Good News. With tears in her eyes, I experienced the joy of leading her to Christ. She emailed me a few days later and said that before we met on the plane, she had all

Saved from suicide!

intentions of committing suicide when she got home! When God knows you will do your best to win someone to Christ, He will guide you to the people He knows are ready to receive Him. You can make a difference, maybe even a life-saving difference!

I was preparing to board a plane from Fargo, North Dakota to Ontario, California returning from a series of meetings in North Dakota. Knowing the plane was a smaller one, claustrophobically seating people 2 by 2, I asked the agent if they had any seats on the plane where I could sit alone. I like to be alone to read, pray or rest. They didn't. Once I got on the plane, I was assigned a seat next to a very large young lady. She too, looking to be more comfortable, moved to another available lone seat before we took off.

I rejoiced and spread my things out on the extra seat, only to have the woman return a few minutes later. I resigned myself to an uncomfortable ride, but subconsciously was familiar with the "arrangements" God sometimes makes at such times, and so I waited to see what would develop.

As I started reading my Bible, I noticed her staring at my personal notes written in the margins. I took advantage of the moment and asked her, "Do you study the Bible?" She replied that she did for catechism training. She was a Lutheran. Yet she admitted that she didn't study it much now. I told her, "You should study the Bible, because Jesus said we are going to be judged by what is written in this book." With that, I began sharing the gospel with her.

As I usually do, I asked her if she had a "born-again experience." She admitted that she had not. I then warned her that Jesus said, "Unless one is born again, he cannot see the kingdom of God" (John 3:3). I further showed that since she had not had that experience, according to God's Word, she couldn't make heaven her home. I continued to show verse after verse explaining this born-again experience.

She soon had questions which needed biblical answers, questions like, "Is homosexuality a sin?" She was a junior in college in Minnesota, studying accounting and had debated such subjects before. It was wonderful to have the plumb line of God's word to measure "every high thing that exalts itself against the knowledge of God" (II Corinthians 10:3-5).

She confessed that she had just that very week thought to herself that she should start getting more serious about church and commented on how "funny" it was that this would happen so close to that decision. She didn't realize that the "Father" was "drawing her" to Christ (John 6:44).

When I finally asked her if she would like to become a born-again Christian and receive Christ, she said "Yes." High flying in the skies over the state of Colorado, this evangelist had the matchless privilege of leading her in repentant prayer. What a joy! I was so glad that the Lord made it inconvenient for me on that trip and supernaturally led a young lady, who was in pursuit of truth, to sit next to me instead of next to one of the other approximately 48 people on that plane!

We must be ready for Spirit-led opportunities to reach out to a dying world. Especially watch for unusual events like a woman changing her seat twice and ending up seated beside you. Such events can be signs from God.

"As many as are led by the Spirit of God, these are the sons of God" (Romans 8:14). Don't be too quick to try to "get away" from an especially talkative stranger, or to get a more comfortable seat somewhere. Don't predetermine to never, ever pick up a hitchhiker. Reject thoughts like, "Oh, they don't know me well enough to want me to visit them in the hospital," etc. Evangelism is never convenient. But then, the cross wasn't convenient, was it?

If you are praying for souls, and have a burden to win souls, then the Lord will surely lead someone into your life at a strategic time in their life. Pray for such occasions, and when they appear, don't miss your opportunity by hiding your light under a bushel (Matthew 5:15). Be a soul-magnet the Holy Spirit can use!

David Kay, 87 years old!

Flying from St. Louis, Missouri home to the Los Angeles area, as usual, I sat near the front at the window. I watched to see who would sit with me until an elderly man named David Kay sat on the isle in my row. Many people passed the open middle seat, which later proved to be an act of God. David and I began to talk immediately. I discovered he really needed to talk.

He had just lost his wife of 69 years and was going to bury her at the Riverside National Cemetery about 60 miles east of Los Angeles. I listened with genuine interest and concern as he talked about his life. He and his wife had traveled the world and had flown lots of places over his many years.

David opened his wallet and showed me the picture of his wife from when she was a high-school cheerleader. Then, he showed me a picture of his loyal dog, and then the Buddha statue in his backyard. He did most of the talking for maybe forty-five minutes. I had won his friendship and gained his trust, so he was ready to listen to me. He had been raised a Catholic. He was now 87 years old and not in the best of health. After a gospel presentation, I led Him to Christ.

Later during the four-hour flight, I asked David if he had anyone to do his graveside service for his wife. He said he didn't. I told him, "I don't live very far from that cemetery. If you would like, I would be happy to drive out to do a committal service for you." He was shocked, "Would you do that?" I assured him I would be happy to. He said, "This is amazing." I don't know how many times he said, "This is amazing." Perhaps for the first time in his life, he was experiencing the goodness and grace of God operating on his behalf.

I performed the service for David's deceased wife in front of maybe a couple of dozen people. I gave David the hope that he would meet his wife in heaven one day. It is a genuine hope since I couldn't judge a woman I had never met. I read Scriptures and shared snippets of the truths of the gospel. Funerals are a captive audience, and I do my best not to take advantage of uninterested people. Afterward, I joined them for a nice meal at the famous Mission Inn in Riverside. Presidents have dined there. He slipped me some money for my services, and after finishing my meal, I left him to visit with his family and friends.

David gave me his phone number, so I called him a week or two later after he had a chance to return home. The person who answered the phone said that he was not feeling well and was in bed. I called another time and left a message which was never returned. I am quite sure that David had died. The thought that I had the privilege of leading him to Christ, perhaps just days before he entered eternity, is staggering to me!

Something David said to me as we were landing at LAX airport touched my heart the most. He had traveled many miles through the years as a representative of the business he co-owned. As he pondered meeting me and what had transpired during that flight, he commented, "I have been on many planes through the years and sat by many people, but this is the first time anything VALUABLE came from it."

In 87 years, only once did David Kay have anything of worth result from all his hours flying on planes.

My brother or sister in Christ, you have something valuable to offer sinners!

Are you offering that "pearl of great price" (Matthew 13:46) to sinners before they die? Or would you rather just look at pictures of their relatives, their dog or their Buddha.

Make the following your ongoing confession,

I have something VALUABLE to offer the world!

I have something VALUABLE to offer the world!

I have something VALUABLE to offer the world!

13

DECADES DEDICATED TO FRIENDS AND FAMILY

"A friend loves at all times and a brother is born to share trouble" (Proverbs 17:17 GW).

As an evangelist, most of my soul-winning opportunities are for a very brief span of time with people I just met for the first time. At most, I will be ministering in a church for a short weekend. But, apart from my job traversing America with the good news, I also have friends and relatives through the years that I have borne a burden for their souls. I share the following stories because I know you have family and friends you long to see find Christ. Be prepared, as I had to be, for what may become a life-long endeavor.

Continue to walk with me on my decades-long journey...

Kenny Johnstone was my very first friend. We attended kindergarten through high school together. He was loyal, and we remained friends throughout our lives. I shared earlier that Kenny was the first person I ever witnessed to but he didn't feel the spiritual need at the time. After months of Bible College training, armed with a better understanding of the

Scriptures, I sat down with him again. I tried to convince him of his need to repent and be born again, pointing out verses that showed we could backslide and we need to get right with the Lord. He didn't know the Bible and couldn't defend himself, so he requested that we head to his church to talk together with his pastor.

Kenny Johnstone 12th grade.

Kenny's parents raised him in a traditional Lutheran Church. Since Kenny was confirmed there and his family attended the church, the Pastor apparently assumed he was saved. But I knew better. I knew Kenny! As I pointed out the Scriptures, the pastor said, "You are talking about sanctification, not salvation." I couldn't get any help from him, and we left with Kenny still unsaved but now feeling that he must be saved. After all, hadn't his pastor said so!

From time to time throughout the years, Kenny would come where I was preaching, partly to honor me and partly because, as he said, I was a "dynamic speaker." Yet he would never acknowledge his need to repent of his sins. He believed in Christ. Wasn't that really all he needed to do? Or so he thought. Eventually, he moved to Louisiana. Sad indeed was the day Kenny visited me after returning to California, announcing that he had stage 4 colon cancer. The doctors gave him at most 24 months with treatment, and 6-12 months without treatment. He chose chemotherapy.

Deeply concerned now for his soul, I called pastors of churches located close to where Kenny lived. Over the next year or so, I scheduled with several churches near his home. I had to fly into Houston, Texas, and then drive about three hours to the area where Kenny lived. He came to the meetings to hear me preach, and I preached to him when he came! He never responded to the altar call, though his teenage son had me baptize him at the church. He was the only person I ever baptized while evangelizing. Kenny and I spent a lot of time together that year. We saw a movie together. We stayed in a motel together, ate together, and even drove around looking at mansions, imagining. I went with him to pick up the dream houseboat he had bought to dock behind their house on the lake where he had built his dream home after retirement. Kenny wanted to spend as much time as he could with his lifelong best friend, and I wanted to see him saved.

The last time I saw Kenny, we sat down at a restaurant in Ontario with other friends from our high school. He was getting weaker and weaker. Apparently, he had been watching Joel Osteen lately. He tried to quote what Joel always leads his congregation and viewers to say on his TV program: "This is my Bible. I am what it says I am. I can do what it says I can do."

Cancer ravaged Kenny's body until his mind was too weak to remember it all, but it delighted me that he had been watching Christian television, and it gave me hope that somehow… That was his last trip to California. His body began filling up with fluids as his liver failed. The doctor put him in hospice for about a week. Then he died at home, almost 24 months after his diagnosis, as the doctors predicted.

I endeavored for over four decades to help Kenny get saved. How many times I prayed for him! I gave seeds of truth to him often. I flew further and drove longer than I ever had before to win anyone's soul to Christ. I hope so much that he is waiting for me in heaven. He will be one of the first ones I look for. There were encouraging signs. Yet, until that day, I can only rest on the promise that Kenny is in the hands of Him who is, "The God of all grace" (1 Peter 5:10). One thing I know for sure, I don't regret one minute that I invested to bring my friend to salvation. I encourage you also to invest time and invest effort in your friend's salvation!

Aunt Bobbie prayed the sinner's prayer in the hospital in the early 1980s, as I shared in Chapter 9. Disappointingly, though, she never started attending church or showed signs of a true conversion. However, I still prayed for her. Decades later, I was preaching in Oregon. Bobbie's house was maybe an hour's drive from my motel, so I drove down to see her. She was now in her late 80s. Like years before, I explained to her the importance of getting right with God. She was very receptive and for the second time, and again prayed the sinner's prayer with me.

Bobbie's bright smile afterward gave me such hope that this time, after decades, it stuck. She died soon thereafter. I'm so glad I invested my time in her soul. Are you ready to invest decades, if need be and the Lord tarrying, to reach out to your relatives?

David Williams, my cousin mentioned several times in earlier chapters, and I were very close, especially during high school. We both got right with God at camp that summer in 1966. However, while I was a freshman in Bible College and he was a senior in high school, he started

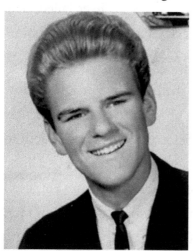

David's 12th grade picture.

running with the wrong crowd and began taking drugs. I visited him often and warned him of his need to get right with the Lord. He asked me once when I thought the Lord would return. I said, "probably within a year". Hey; I was only a half-a-century or so off, not bad for a new theologian in training!

David came and heard me preach sometimes. He even came down to the altar to get right with God one evening…

but those drugs! Through the years, I visited him and kept urging him to surrender to the Lord. He knew he wasn't right with God. Eventually, he not only took drugs, but he also began selling them from his living room. He enjoyed the ride until two thugs entered his house and robbed him at gunpoint. He then sold his home to move his young family to a safer area, yet still not surrendering to Christ.

Wandering from one place to another, and from this job to that one, David finally settled in an apartment in Las Vegas, working part-time as he found work. I prayed for him, and I worried about him. When at last I received an opportunity to speak in a church in Las Vegas, I called David and asked him if I could pick him up to go to church with me. He was happy to do so. My mother also was with me that day. David and his teenage son, Stephen, sat in the service. To my joy, they both raised their hands at my invitation to get right with God. Soon they were down at the altar, father and son, praying for forgiveness.

I can still visualize David on one knee, with one arm raised heavenward to the Lord that his preacher father, my Uncle Marvin, had raised him to fear.

That afternoon, we ate KFC chicken together at David's apartment. He had lost all his teeth by then because of a lifetime of drugs. He couldn't afford false teeth. I watched amazed as he gummed chicken off the bones. We had a lot of catching up to do. Before I left, I took his picture and I urged David to follow the Lord and get back to church. I then drove away.

My last picture of cousin, David, standing beside my late mother.

Within two months, David died of a heart attack, while still but in his 50's. I believe the Lord took David home, because of His grace, because of the prayers of his godly father, and because of my prayers and my witness. I also believe the Lord took him because he knew that he would not live the life.

"...many of you are weak and sick, and quite a few have died. But if we had judged ourselves, we wouldn't be judged. However, we are disciplined by the Lord when we are judged so that we won't be judged and condemned along with the whole world" (1 Corinthians 11:30-32).

You can imagine, after hearing of David's sudden death, how grateful I was that during my entire adult life I continued to pursue him, and I took time to take him to church with me while he still had a few months left on earth. Do you have relatives and friends who still have time? Pray, call, and invite them to church. Never give up on them, and then what a reunion you'll have in heaven.

The Abell Family lived a few houses down from our house on Maple Street. I was four years old when our family moved to our home in Ontario, California directly across the street from Kenny. The Abell's had the biggest family I had ever seen: 2 parents, 8 boys, and 2 girls. Three of the boys were about my age and we played often together. The following stories are about my friends Eddie, Jessie, and Larry.

Eddie Abell was a year or so ahead of me. One summer, he went to Vacation Bible School with me. In our small Sunday School room, our teacher cried as she warned (and terrified!) a table full of kids about the coming Great Tribulation. Guess who was soon on their knees repenting: Eddie and me! We didn't want any antichrist cutting off our heads! Every Church should be blessed today with such wise children's workers!

Jessie Abell was near my age too. He fell off of their garage roof and hit his head on the pavement below. The accident left him mentally handicapped, with a metal plate in his head. One of my mom's favorite stories of my childhood concerned Jessie.

A church I attended sometimes, where my sister was a member, had a Christmas party and a gift exchange for the children. I wanted Jessie to go with me. The problem was, with a family of 12, they had little money, so he couldn't buy a gift. In order for Jessie to go with me, I took a bunch of my old comic books and wrapped them up in a box with gift-wrapping for Jessie to bring along as his gift. When I returned home from church later, mother roared with laughter upon seeing me carrying in my gift from the exchange: a box of my old comic books!

Larry Abell, in my same class in grammar school, was my closest friend of all his family. He walked with me to the little church where I got saved in the second grade. At that same altar where I was first saved, Larry also knelt and asked Jesus to become his Savior. His unsaved family could not provide any encouragement to him, so he fell away. In our sophomore year of high school, his family moved to Springfield, Oregon. In my mind, I can still see the Abell's car crammed full, with two parents and a number of kids headed away from Maple Street to their new home. I didn't see any of them again for many years.

During the time I served as a youth minister in Crescent City in northern California, Larry Abell and his wife drove up the California coast to their home in Oregon. He found out I lived nearby, and he called me. I invited them to stay with us for a few days. They did. As in our younger days, Larry and I had fun together again, talking, strolling the beach. They came to church on Sunday morning, and Larry answered the pastor's altar call. I knelt beside him to help him pray. I was delighted with his decision to rededicate his life to Christ.

We lost track of one another until I was preaching decades later in Oregon. I found the Abell's phone number in the phone book and called to tell them I would love to come by and see them. They were happy to invite me. Larry's mother was deceased, but his father and most of the kids were there at their dad's house when I arrived to visit. After reliving old times, I preached the gospel to them all and most of them prayed the sinner's prayer with me. I am sure some of them said the prayer just to honor me, but Larry was among those repenting, for at least the third time in his life.

Unfortunately, Larry was an alcoholic and never established himself in a church. Years later, I was preaching in an Assembly of God Church in the Saint Louis area. While in the sanctuary after speaking, I received a phone call from Larry's daughter. She explained that Larry was in the hospital in very poor health, but he requested to see me. I told her I would do my best. Fortunately, I had enough miles with United to fly round trip to Eugene, Oregon as soon as I returned from my services in Missouri.

Eddie picked me up at the airport and broke the bad news that Larry had very little time to live. We drove straight to the hospital. I walked into his room where Larry was alert and glad to see me. His organs were all shutting down from advanced alcoholism! We experienced quite a reunion as we once again relived old times. Then, I got down to business and talked to him about his soul. Larry knew he was dying, and that is why he wanted me to come. I explained again what he needed to do and led him back to the Lord for the fourth time!

I started describing heaven, seeking to give him some hope in his final hours on earth. Larry's brother, Eddie, walked into the hospital room. The first thing Larry told Eddie was, "Hey, Eddie! Dea told me they have food in heaven!" Anybody who has eaten hospital food can appreciate that one!

Soon, Larry drifted off to sleep. His vital signs were relatively stable, so Eddie took me to my motel for some sleep. However, a few hours later, Eddie phoned my room and awakened me, reporting that the nurses warned the family that Larry's condition was deteriorating rapidly. He had very little time left. We pensively drove together to the hospital.

Larry slipped into a coma with nothing more they could do. Unusual experiences occurred that night. Because it was a Catholic Hospital, a nun came in to comfort the family. As they stood around Larry's bed in the room, she sang hymns and played her guitar. It seemed to me that the family did not appreciate this stranger's intrusion on their final moments with their close family member, especially not being Catholics. Also, the hospital had the weirdest video playing on the TV in the room. It showed white lights (representing spirits?) rising slowly upward towards heaven to join many other lights (angels?). I suppose the nuns sincerely thought somehow that helped the family believe and visualize Larry soon joining those lights. But along with the eerie sound tract playing, it certainly was something I had never seen before.

As I stood at his bedside, I watched as Larry's breathing became more and more labored. Then it became as though his spirit was desperately trying to stay in his body. The muscles in his chest strained as hard as they could. His mouth and chin opened and closed, slowly, then even more slowly. Yet no air appeared to enter his lungs. Then he was gone. In that moment, Larry's eyes, which had been closed, opened widely. They seemed fixed, staring toward the heavens, almost as though Larry could see his spirit rising. His now-grown son closed Larry's eyes in death.

I comforted the family as best I could, hugging them all and saying our goodbyes. The next morning, I flew home. Family members told me later that they scattered Larry's ashes in the river where he loved to fish. Larry died. Jessie died of cancer. Their brother Jerry, who was older, had gotten gloriously saved, attended church, and wouldn't even allow his brothers to drink in his house! Not my witness, but somebody else reached Jerry!

Jerry died of cancer. Their father died. The other older brothers died. One by one, they all moved from Maple Street, on to Oregon, and

finally to heaven or hell. Of the twelve, only four of the Abell family members remain on earth. I pray for each one of them, by name, every day!

By the grace of God, Larry is in heaven. Nevertheless, the Lord needed a little help from an evangelist; his time, his ministry's money, and his air miles to help an old dear friend, for the fourth time

Larry Abell, a life-long project.

spanning across decades, to prepare for eternity.

The Lord may soon need a little help from you also. Help your dear friends and relatives get ready for eternity. Take the initiative to keep in touch with them. Pray for them daily. Share the truth of the gospel with them when you can. Invite them to church and Christian gatherings.

Until you have done, as best as is humanly possible, your God-ordained personal evangelism assignment, contend for their souls with a passion that…

God won't let them die until they are saved!

14

MY 50TH HIGH SCHOOL REUNION

**"Young people, enjoy your youth. Be happy while you are still
young. Do what you want to do, and follow your
heart's desire. But remember that God is going to judge
you for whatever you do" (Ecclesiastes 11:9 GNT).**

Chaffey High school, Ontario, California, less than 40 miles east of
downtown Los Angeles, was and is still one of the biggest high schools in
the state with 3,500 students. The campus is one of the largest as well
covering 65 acres. Over 900 students were in my freshman class alone!

In 2017, about 150 of the class of 1967 showed up for our 50th
reunion. Interestingly, during much of that half-a-century, I had dreams
during the night of being back in classes at Chaffey or at least being with
students in my class. I told one alumnus this, and she said she continued
to have dreams too about being at Chaffey, but for her, they were
nightmares. I asked her if she was insecure in school, and she admitted
she was. I don't believe my dreams were only the subconscious memories
of the joys of those years or because I missed my senior year, as one person
suggested. I believe my subconscious dreams might have stemmed from

being the only one in the class called to be an evangelist, and I sought to do the work of an evangelist at that reunion. Though so many of my classmates obviously didn't know the Lord, I did. I thanked God at this reunion that I am saved by His grace.

I was amazed to see how much we all had changed. For five decades, when I looked in the mirror, I saw a teenager with wrinkles on his face. Apparently, that wasn't what my fellow 1967 classmates saw. For instance, while standing near a man I didn't recognize, I asked him his name. He said, "Tim." I said, "Tim who?" He replied, "Orr." I exulted, "Tim! It's Dea Warford!" and we hugged!

Tim and I had been friends and both attended the same elementary school through Jr. High and High School. All these years later, we stood next to each other and still didn't recognize one another! What a shock to me! Tim remarked that when he saw my name on the reunion registry he

I'm on the left with some of my fellow Chaffey Tigers, and NO, I do NOT have a beer in my hand!

told someone, "Dea Warford. I want to see him!" He even said I was just one of two people he looked forward to seeing. But he had aged so much I couldn't even recognize him. . . uh, then again, he couldn't recognize me either! So much for a wrinkled teenage face!

Most of our former classmates were by then gray or white- headed. Like me, many of the girls refused to accept old age and dyed their hair. If God wanted me to have gray hair, I figure He wouldn't have created dye! Some of the cutest girls in the school were still the cutest, at least to me! (They might not have been to a 17-year-old, though). Quite a few of the athletes, class officers, and cheerleaders I once wished to date also attended the reunion. After seeing me at 68, I bet those cheerleaders were sorry now! Many had certainly changed and several used canes or limped. Some had gained weight and some were still skinny. Most of us surely looked our age! To rub our age in further, for our 55th reunion they are planning to have a luncheon so we won't have to drive at night! Oh, how Ecclesiastes 12:1 had come to pass, "Remember now thy creator in the days of thy youth while the evil days come not" (KJV).

The aging process is indeed a great evil. . . especially when gifted with a face like mine! People tell me I don't look my age. Now I realize they probably mean: "You don't look 71, maybe 70!"

I carry many memories of Chaffey. Some aren't good. I was in a number of fights and usually lost! I wasn't much of an athlete. I never held a class office. Cheerleaders? Never dated one. Nor was I Prom King, Homecoming King, or voted Most Likely to Succeed. Yet, I do carry many other pleasant memories: I dated a lot of girls, had many friends, and was part of the surfer crowd for a while. Ocean, sun, and fun…those were the days!

Ever heard of the Vestels rock band? Well, I played a B-3 organ with them. Competing against nine other bands, we won the "Battle of the Bands" at the Oasis Teen Club dance. The Vestels became an excellent band and eventually played for a Los Angeles television program. That didn't happen, though, until after a couple of talent agents recommended they get rid of me, which they were happy to do!

Thanks to God's creative gift, I was an excellent student. In my freshman year, I got a prophetic glimpse into the fact that I would one day be a writer. I wrote a story, and the English teacher read it aloud to her classes as exemplary writing. I was also usually the class clown. In fact, someone brought our De Anza Junior High annual, now politically corrected to middle school. It was from 1963 and had a picture of me with the inscription, "School Wit."

As I look back on my life, it should have said "half-wit!"

Speaking of the gift of wit, one funny memory of my Chaffey years occurred when school leaders were searching for a new name for the "Shipwreck Hop," which Chaffey hosted annually. Kids dressed up in Hawaiian or beach garb for the evening of fun. I submitted a name that they chose: "Moby Dick and His Chick." I won two free tickets to the dance for that one!

Another time, I spoke for a chapel service at a Christian College in Virginia. After hearing me speak to the students and seeing my mixed bag of hilarity and solemnity, the college president said, "I believe the Lord gave you your sense of humor because you have such a hard message." I trust he meant hard-hitting, not hard to take! My sense of humor has assisted me wonderfully in witnessing. I endeavor to show people the joy of the Lord and that Christianity can be fun. Proverbs 17:22, "A merry heart does good like a medicine," is certainly true and I have discovered that humor can help people to more easily swallow the gos...pill.

If you aren't gifted in making people laugh, you can still make them happy! Smile often, compliment them generously, and show love for all sinners. Also, continually soften hard to take words like Satan, hell, or repentance by always including more soothing words like Jesus, heaven, and grace.

Use wisdom at all times! One time, in a convenience market, I heard a zealous Christian trying to preach to everyone in the store, that is, to anybody who would listen to him. I watched in silence, waiting at my place in line while he forced the two workers behind the counter to pay attention to him. One worker, trying to inject a little lightheartedness to the embarrassing moment, added an off-handed joke to the one-sided conversation. The zealot rebuked him saying, "This is no time to try to be funny. This is serious business!" The witness made a monkey out of himself. If he had any wisdom at all, he would have shown a little more respect for an employee.

Sinner's loved being around Jesus. We want sinners to enjoy being around us too!

Back to my class reunion. To my knowledge, I am the only one in the class preaching the gospel full-time, and I am surely the only evangelist. This fact gave me a great sense of responsibility at the reunion. I don't know when I have felt a greater burden for souls. I prayed daily and asked God to lead me, anoint me, and give me wisdom for soul-winning. I handed out some tracts, witnessed when the door seemed to open, and gave my testimony of how I found the Lord. It wasn't an ideal time to witness. Almost always other people were nearby or interrupting to visit with the person to whom I was talking.

I was very disappointed that I didn't get to lead someone to Christ. I tried though – tried hard! But I did spend time talking with a Buddhist.

Another intellectual type asked me challenging questions that I did my best to answer. Remember, we are talking about 68-year-olds pretty settled in their beliefs. I heard in Bible College that the odds of someone getting saved after 60 years of age are only 1 in a million! Thank God we have the truth that, "with God all things are possible" (Matthew 10:27).

The saddest part of the reunion occurred during the banquet. A DVD player and TV Screen continually played in a corner of the banquet area,

Jane Hinson

slowly displaying, one by one, the names and graduation pictures of our classmates who had died. Their pictures reminded us that they were just kids, full of hope for a bright future, which they were unable to fulfill.

Among them was the second girl I ever kissed, in 1st grade, Jan Hinson. She was killed in a car accident years back. I remember her and her boyfriend stopping for a while at the LA County Fair to listen to me preach the gospel to a crowd of maybe 40 or so people who gathered to see and hear this extraordinary sight before the police came and made me stop! I hope that moment of witness helped her make a decision for Christ before she died! Perhaps God had inspired me to speak that day for her sake.

Gerald Dubois

My all-time best friend Kenny Johnstone's picture also scrolled past. Few people knew the lengths I had gone to help him come to the Lord, but my Judge, Jesus knew!

Gerald DuBois was a good friend in Jr. High. I was Jr. High President one semester, and Gerald was President the next. He died over a decade earlier of an unusual disease wherein iron settled in the body, slowly killing him. I wish I had made the effort to visit him and win him to Christ. I hadn't even heard that he was sick. If I'd known he would die, I'd have gone to his hospital bed to assure both me and him of his readiness to meet the Lord. Of course, we don't know when people will die, do we? That's why we must be diligent witnesses! In front of the televised memorial, I knelt for a moment and asked God to help me to win souls before they die! What a responsibility! Prepare for your next reunion, family get-together, or other celebration to do the work of an evangelist.

Randy Huntington came to Camp Cedar Crest with our church youth group when I was Youth Minister at the Upland Foursquare Church. After several days at camp and several altar calls, he hadn't made a decision for Christ yet. I talked to him in our cabin about the urgency of doing so. He replied, "I'll wait until I get old." Well, he never got old. I don't know how or when he died, but if he continued to wait, I'm sure he is now in hell.

Randy Huntington

I didn't deserve to be chosen to be among the "few that are saved" (Luke 12: 23, 24). I was a great sinner in school, a worse sinner, by far than many other students. Why should I get to go to heaven while so many of my fellow classmates won't? It's truly an enigma! We could argue the theology involved in this. All I know for sure is that, like Paul the Apostle, "I am a debtor" (Romans 1:14-16). I owed it, like a debt, to my unsaved fellow-classmates to point them to Christ!

I came to the many sessions of the reunion with a weight on my shoulders. I even found myself sweating as I drove to one event. I felt an awesome responsibility and realization that many of these "Tigers," I would never see again. That is, until they stand before the Lord and millions of other Christians at the judgment seat of Christ (1 Corinthians 6:2). Some of them might not live until our 55th class reunion. I might be their best chance to get saved.

My brother and sister, though you may not feel such a sense of "last opportunity" that I felt during this 50th reunion, you may have only one last opportunity to witness to some lost soul. Do it!

The second evening of the reunion fellow classmate Sandy Jarvis, now known as Sam Upton, a Christian friend and supporter of my ministry, stopped me and looked me seriously in the eyes. She said, "I've heard reports from other Tigers from the previous night that Dea was now, 'wonderful and gentle.'" No one during my high school years ever said I was "wonderful" and certainly not "gentle." Thankfully, after decades of spiritual growth, and by Christ's transforming power, those who "knew me when" could see the transforming power of Christ in me!

The "Wonderful Counselor" (Isaiah 9:6) delivered me from so many character flaws from my past. The Galatians 5:22-24 "fruit of the Spirit . . . gentleness" had slowly but surely grown in me. Her words gave me a sliver of encouragement wedged between many other disappointments that weekend. The Lord knew I needed a little comfort.

As an evangelist, I am very results-oriented. I want to be like the prototype Phillip whose ministry brought quick and great city-wide results (Acts 8:4-8). Pastors are more patient and plodding in their work. Though I didn't see my desire fulfilled by leading my classmates to Christ, still God had seen how badly I wanted to be used by Him and how dissatisfied I was with the results. So loving God that He is, He made sure that I at least found out from my friend, Sam, that my "labor [was] not in vain in the Lord" (1 Corinthians 15:58).

I was apparently, at least in some measure, a fulfillment of Jesus' words, "You are the light of the world . . . let your light so shine before men that they may see your works and glorify the Father" (John 5:15,16). Soul-winning can be very difficult and at times frustrating. Yet if you, as I did at a once-in-a-lifetime 50th class reunion, fail in any attempt to lead someone to Christ, you can at least still keep shining for Jesus. You can be a bright point of light in an ever-increasingly darkening world.

God revealed to me decades ago that my ministry was primarily for the closing days of time. I really believe that! During the greatest difficulties of all time and the greatest spiritual movement of all time, I want to be a person my fellow Chaffey "Tigers" will remember! When, "Men's hearts [will be] failing them from fear and the expectation of those things which are coming on the earth, for the powers of the heavens will be shaken" (Luke 21:26), I want them to know I am an available spiritual resource to them. I hope many reach out to me for help and find Christ before it is too late. I've made myself easy to find on Facebook or at my website. And I do not have an unlisted phone number. Call me now if I can lead you to Christ: 918-576-4680!

Carry your cross of disappointment. Continue to hold the realistic hope that one day your witness and light-filled representation of God's love will result in an old friend or classmate saying, "I know who can help me now! It's that fanatical Christian that was always preaching to me!"

Do you think I'm being too idealistic? I am not! You have the prophet's promise of this.

"...darkness shall cover the earth, And deep darkness the people; But the Lord will arise over you, And His glory will be seen upon you. The Gentiles SHALL COME TO YOUR LIGHT, and the kings to the brightness of your rising" (Isaiah 60:2, 3).

Let "His glory be seen upon you" always, and especially when sinners are around you. Make yourself fully available to them. Then, according to Isaiah, one day…

They "shall come to your light."

15

MANY DISAPPOINTMENTS: ONE GREAT VICTORY

"I will take no pleasure in anyone who turns away. But we are not like those who turn away from God to their own destruction. We are the faithful ones, whose souls will be saved" (Hebrews 10:38, 39 NLT).

I have pointed out to you many milestones in my soul-winning journey. I hope they have encouraged you. But I must be completely transparent. Evangelism is often difficult for me, and victories are tempered by many apparent defeats.

Just as I've experienced joyful moments, I have also experienced many disappointments on this journey, as at my 50th reunion. Jesus warned us to "count the cost" (Luke 14:28). Winning souls comes with a price to pay. Are you willing to pay that price? If you think you are, prepare yourself for...

Persecution... something all Christians must be prepared to face, especially as we wage war on the frontlines of evangelism and as we approach the Last Days. Persecution will surely increase (Matthew 10:21, 22).

Thus far, I haven't faced serious persecution. However, one time, while preaching to a small group of youth in front of Knott's Berry Farm in Buena Park, California, one of the boys sucker-punched me. People have sneered at me, slammed doors on me, and things like that, but compared to evangelists and missionaries in third world countries who have been imprisoned, tortured or killed, my sufferings are not worthy to be compared with theirs.

Regret... I know for a fact that many people will be in hell forever and ever, not just for their own sin, but because I failed to fulfill my obligation to the Lord to "take up the cross" of evangelism (Matt. 10:39). My first insight into this grim reality occurred when I came home one weekend from college to spend time with my parents. My dad loved to drink wine, and to my mother's loathing, had many drinking buddies. He often invited different ones over to the house so they could visit and drink together. One evening, as I played a religious song on the piano, one of Dad's drinking buddies came over to show how religious he was. It is amazing how religious a person can become when they are drunk! He told the story of a little "colored boy" who was sitting on the steps outside of a church. Jesus walked by and said, "What's wrong son?" The boy said, "They won't let me in there!" Jesus told him, "That's OK son, they won't let me in there either." It was a touching story, especially during the Civil Rights Movement. I felt the strongest urge to say to him, "And that same Jesus wants to come into your heart." But I didn't. Why? He was drunk. He was boisterous. He was disgusting, and I figured he probably wouldn't receive it anyway, so why bother.

The next day, my father broke the news to me that the man died in a car accident. The thought that he was burning in hell at that very moment was difficult, and especially hard to realize that I had probably been the last person who could have helped him. The call of the evangelist had urged me to witness, but I failed in the task. This was a lesson I never forgot, yet often repeated nevertheless!

I must be honest, I don't expect some great reward in heaven for the souls I have won to Christ. Why? Because I could have won so many more if I had just been less selfish, more obedient, more loving. It is one thing to regret not getting more education, saving more money, helping out at the church more. It is quite another to regret not doing my part to "save a soul from death" (James 5:20).

Disappointment... can be very discouraging for any Christian or ministry when hopes, prayers, and hard work do not appear to bear fruit. This has certainly been true in my life as an evangelist.

Those who turn away from God... Gary Sexton, you might remember, was the teenager I led to Christ when I was in youth ministry. Before he married or went to LIFE, he came to live with my wife and me for several months while we pastored in Walla Walla, Washington. We talked a lot. One day, he shared with me that he had been experiencing a strong temptation while he was in our town. He said he even drove past the place at times, the pull was so alluring. He wouldn't tell me what it was, and I had no idea. Then one day, the Lord revealed to me that it was homosexuality. I asked him about that, and he totally denied it.

Then he went off to Bible College and met and married his wife there. They had a son together and lived in the Midwest. Gary drove out to California. He admitted to me that he was there to "study" homosexuality. He planned to visit gay bars to interact with men but assured me that he would tell them he was remaining celibate. Then he admitted that he struggled with homosexual feelings much of his life, as God had revealed to me earlier. As a Christian, he knew he couldn't yield to those urges and chose to pursue a heterosexual life.

Gary attended a state college for further study. I am quite sure liberal academic attitudes toward sexuality began to poison his mind. He even visited with one of his professors in his apartment. They drank together and later Gary awakened from a deep sleep and knew he had been violated. He figured the professor must have slipped him a mickey. Unsatisfied with his marriage, he had decided to explore the dark side! You likely know what developed. He met Bill, "fell in love," divorced his wife, left his son without a father, and "married" a man.

Through the years, we occasionally talked on the phone, though the joy no longer existed. He stopped attending church. He knew they wouldn't accept his lifestyle, as this was decades ago. To justify leaving the church he told me, "The church is the only army that shoots its wounded." I later thought of a comeback, "But every army shoots their traitors." He had become a traitor to his wife, his God, and his Bible. He convinced himself that he was saved because "by grace are you saved through faith" (Ephesians 2:8). But, he had apparently forgotten that "faith without works is dead" (James 2:26).

Sadly, Bill hadn't told his new "husband" that he had AIDS. Before long, Gary also developed AIDS. His wife called to give me the tragic report of his death. There was no evidence that Gary ever repented of his homosexual sin.

Sometime later, I remembered a story that Gary had told me. His ex-wife was away at a women's camp, so he and a male friend drove 35 miles one-way to rent a VCR and pornographic videos. When they returned home and put the videos in the VCR, they discovered the VCR was broken. I believe the Lord, in his great mercy, was giving Gary an opportunity to repent. God even gave Jezebel an opportunity to repent in Revelation 2:20, 21. Unfortunately, like Jezebel, Gary refused God's moment of grace. Instead, he and his friend drove 35 miles one-way again to switch VCRs and over a hundred miles later viewed the videos together and the Lord only knows what else went on that night.

Gary chose to resist the grace of God and stubbornly refused to follow what 1 Corinthians 10:12 says, "Let him who thinks he stands take heed lest he fall." I believe God was fulfilling His promise in the very next verse, "God is faithful, who will not allow you to be tempted beyond what you are able, but with the temptation will also make the way to escape" (1 Corinthians 10:13). The VCR was broken. He knew the ways of God enough to know that this was a sign. He was not a new convert. He studied the Bible for years at LIFE. He read the warning, "If we sin willfully after we have received the knowledge of the truth, there no longer remains a sacrifice for sins, but a certain fearful expectation of judgment, and fiery indignation" (Hebrews 10:22, 27).

Homosexual urges are not what damn a person's soul. Yielding to and then repeatedly, defiantly acting on those urges brings the condemnation, "Neither fornicators...nor adulterers, nor homosexuals, nor sodomites...will inherit the kingdom of God" (1 Corinthians 16:9). Hate the sin, but love the sinner. Never compromise truth in your zeal to see homosexuals saved. Gary's fall from grace (Galatians 5:4) stands as one of my most bitter disappointments as an evangelist. But there is one disappointment even more bitter to me which involved my nephew.

Shane was my brother, Eddie's, firstborn son. When my nephew was in grammar school, sometimes I drove by to pick him up and take him to Sunday school and church with me. During his high school years, he began to run with the wrong crowd and started getting in trouble. My brother, hoping to move him physically out of the area, called and asked me if Shane could come and live with my wife and me in Walla Walla. We didn't have any children yet, so we agreed. As I recall, he rode the bus from Ontario to Washington and lived with us for a semester.

Shane came to the services with us, listened to my sermons, but never responded to the altar call. Years later, he met a girl named Kathy, fell in

Shane, Kathy, and their first child.

love, and asked me to perform their wedding ceremony. I was happy to, and it was a wonderful family affair. He had a good job, and they bought their own home. They had three children together. But over time, Shane eventually grew bitter against his wife, and his heart filled with unforgiveness. I invited Shane to lunch with me, and I did my best to convince him to forgive Kathy and keep his family together. He remained resolute. He could not and would not forgive her. As I drank a coke, I pointed down to his beer and told him, "You know, that alcohol is the big stumbling block in your life." My brother and his wife were both alcoholics, and the children had been raised watching them drink. His mom died of alcoholism! I urged him to repent of drinking, forgive his wife, go to church, and get right with the Lord. He refused.

Shane's wife, Kathy, became distraught over all this. She loved Shane, begged his forgiveness, and did her best to try to keep the family together. I invited her to talk with me. As we sat on the lawn at her mother's house, I tried to console her. Then, I shared the gospel with her. She knew she needed the Lord's help more than ever, and she received Christ. She was born again! Kathy went on to faithfully follow the Lord and remarried. Her new husband was an assistant pastor. Kathy and I visit on the phone from time to time. I pray for her daily! She had a happy ending, but Shane…

Shane lost his job and eventually became a homeless drunk. He and his girlfriend, Rita, often slept behind trash bins and he stood on a corner holding a cardboard sign. Receiving handouts paid for their daily alcohol consumption. From time-to-time, Shane and Rita came to where I preached in Ontario. I have a picture after one service when Shane answered the altar call to get right with God. In the picture, Shane is all smiles and his proud uncle was so happy. Unfortunately, he didn't really repent, and he still wasn't willing to forsake the bottle.

From time-to-time, I talked with Shane and encouraged him to get right with God, get baptized, go to church, or go to Alcoholics Anonymous. I told him I would happily tie the knot, so their sleeping together would be legal. But, he wouldn't budge. They eventually found a trailer park to live in. Since they had an actual address, I mailed them my monthly newsletter, hoping my "Sermon of the Month" might get a hold of them.

The newsletter listed church locations where I was scheduled to preach. Shane saw that I was going to be at the Cabazon, California Foursquare Church. I was still his favorite uncle, and he enjoyed listening to me preach. His trailer park was located just off the freeway heading from where I lived in Santa Fe Springs. He called and asked if I would pick him and Rita up so they could go to church with me. I, of course, was happy to oblige. Soon they sat in the small congregation while I was on the platform preaching.

Shane and Rita were the only unsaved listening to me that day. I preached on hell. I was likely the only preacher within a 50-mile radius preaching the whole message on hell that morning. Sermons like that can drive away tithers! I did something that morning I almost never do. I preached my sermon directly to two people, my nephew, and his live-in girlfriend. I described hell as the Bible describes it; hot, horrible, eternal. When I gave the altar call, I watched the two carefully, hoping they would raise their hands. I pulled and I pulled for that result but in vain.

After the service, the pastor, Shane and Rita, and I all went out for lunch together. I dropped them off back at the trailer park. That was the last time I ever saw Shane. Within a couple of weeks, I received a phone call from Rita. She had been away for a few days, and when she returned home, she found Shane dead on the floor of the trailer, surrounded by empty bottles after a weekend of drinking. Neither Rita nor Shane's three children had the money for a proper burial. Shane was cremated without even a memorial service. "Let me die the death of the righteous" (Numbers 23:10).

I often think about Shane. I can't help but picture him weeping, wailing, and gnashing his teeth in the flames of hell, so regretting that he didn't listen to his uncle. But, I have few regrets. I drove out of my way to pick him up for Sunday School when he was little. I let him live with us to help him out while in high school. I took him out to lunch and counseled him to forgive and keep his family together. Again, and again, I urged him to get right with God. One time I did succeed in getting him down to the altar to repent. But I couldn't keep him on the straight and narrow path.

I am grateful that I had one last opportunity with Shane. I picked him up as a child a half-century earlier to take him to church with me. I preached with all my heart. I urged him one last time to repent of his sins and get right with God.

Maybe the Lord dealt with Shane one last time in that trailer. Maybe he had awakened in the morning, with his mind relatively cleared of the effects of alcohol. Did he glance around the trailer at the poverty he brought upon himself? Did he stare with contempt at the expensive, now empty bottles? Because he knew exactly what he needed to do, did he one more time kneel on that trailer living room floor and repent of drunkenness, "Do you not know that the unrighteous will not inherit the kingdom of God?...nor drunkards" (1 Corinthians 6:9, 10). Did he, like the publican on the hilltop, cry, "God be merciful to me a sinner" (Luke 18:13)?

Did "the God of all grace" (1 Peter 5:10) in that very moment, knowing that Shane would never break free from alcohol, take him "scarcely saved" into His presence? (1 Peter 4:1). I fear the worst for Shane, yet I still hope for the best. Were his uncle's prayers at last answered? If so, Shane will be one of my greatest, and most appreciated surprises when I get to heaven! We serve "The God of hope" (Romans 15:13).

I believe in death-bed conversions. I have looked into the eyes of a dying man and seen the dread of death. He was in the hospital, knowing he didn't have long to live. He wanted to speak to a preacher. I was pastoring nearby, so a nurse gave me a call. I rushed up there, needless to say. He listened intently as I told him, "Whoever calls upon the name of the Lord shall be saved" (Romans 10:13). He called upon Jesus' Precious Name that very night. I expect to see him in heaven.

Those who reject our witness or accept it and then later turn from it, hence losing out on eternity, are a soul-winner's greatest cause for mourning, "I shall mourn for many who have sinned before and have not repented of the uncleanness, fornication, and licentiousness which they have practiced" (2 Corinthians 12:21).

Yes, I have had many disappointments in this life-long work of an evangelist. Nonetheless, the joys make it all worthwhile. The eternal rewards mitigate the disappointments. I will never regret my many efforts to take Gary Sexton and Shane Warford with me to heaven. I promise, you also will not regret ANY efforts you make when you do the work of an evangelist.

One Victory… Last night, the Lord reminded me in the middle of the night of a story I had neglected to put in this book. I think after sad stories like the above, this would be a great place to add the following memory.

Mary broke up with me in 1967, and I moped about for a few weeks. Then, I remembered Cheryl Rackley, a beautiful blue-eyed, natural blonde I knew from my childhood. Her grandmother lived next door to us, and during summers she stayed with her grandma. Kenny and I often played sports out front trying to impress her as she sat on her grandma's porch. Cheryl and I kind of liked each other and even kissed a few times.

I was alone again and needed a girlfriend, desperately! Cheryl, at that time, lived in Reseda with her mother and her brother. That was like being a continent away from my childhood home, but I now had my own car! Her house was only 20 or so miles away from the college. I decided to drive to see her again and maybe…?

After knocking at Cheryl's door and seeing her for the first time in years, she invited me into her living room. Cheryl and her younger brother, Bob, and I visited for quite a while. Before long I knew this was too opportune of a time for me not to share the gospel with them. Again, as I had so many times before, I walked them through the steps of the "Encounter Method" that Pastor Jack taught me. I wasn't very far into the presentation when Cheryl, under such conviction of sin, cried out, "But how do I get saved?" Pastor Jack hadn't taught me what to do if they wouldn't even let me finish! I asked her to just listen to me until I was done. Afterward, she received Christ.

I phoned her not long afterward to see how she was doing spiritually. She was discouraged and admitted that she was backsliding. I had given her a booklet specifically written for new converts. I asked her if she had read that book yet. She admitted she hadn't. I replied, "Cheryl, you have got to read that book!" giving her the strongest urging possible. She read the book and her life was suddenly transformed.

The promises of the Bible, the assurance of salvation that was explained in that booklet, enlightened her soul. She didn't have to backslide. She didn't have to be depressed about life. She was saved! She became a strong witness for the Lord, gave away all her miniskirts (this was the 1960s!) and soon was President of the youth group where she started attending church. Her brother Bob serves Christ today as a worship leader. Their mother died a child of God!

I asked Cheryl to share her testimony. Here it is in her words:

"A few days later, Dea called to ask if I'd read the booklet he'd given me. I think the name was, "What Every New Convert Should Know." I was fighting a cold and in bed early, so I promised I'd read it that night. As I read the Scriptures, my room filled with the tangible presence of God. "You're real!" I exclaimed, shocked, and delighted at God's reality. From that moment, all desire I had to sin fell away. It was an immediate and thorough conversion that set the foundation that would hold me throughout the rest of life's challenges. I'm now almost seventy and can say that although I've failed many times, He has never failed me. My father died early of lung cancer but gratefully received Christ. He died full of the joy of the Lord. My brother Larry also found faith in Jesus before he died. And my grandfather, both grandmothers. In fact, we've not lost, one who has died without knowing the Savior. This is by His great grace. Like Dea, I believe the Lord is kind to visit His children on their deathbeds, so never give up hope that your loved one might certainly be waiting in heaven when you arrive."

Cheryl came to one of my meetings nearly two decades ago when I was preaching in Ashland, Oregon. We've kept in touch ever since. I believe the Lord quickened her memory to my heart so that I could end what could have been a very discouraging chapter with an encouraging story. Yes, some will fall away from the faith, sadly. However, others, like Cheryl kept the faith, and her entire family will one day be all reunited in heaven.

I wanted a girlfriend that day as I drove the LA freeways to Cheryl's house. The Lord had something very different in mind. He wanted me to become a father in the faith!

You too can become a father or mother in the faith by learning a gospel presentation and then giving it away! Yes, there will be many disappointments along your soul-winning journey, but I promise you it will be worth it all if you only achieve...

One Great Victory!

16

YOU DON'T HAVE TO PREACH!

"And I keep praying that this faith we hold in common
keeps showing up in the good things we do, and
that people recognize Christ in all of it"
(Philemon 1:6 MSG).

When I was a younger evangelist, I thought everybody should be like me. I thought every Christian should share the gospel, do it regularly, and do it often. I must make something very clear. I would absolutely love to see you boldly preaching the gospel and frequently leading souls to Christ. But, and I mean this sincerely, for most Christians that will be a very infrequent experience.

God does NOT expect you to try to turn every conversation, or every apparent open door, into a soul-winning sermon. Yet, He does want you to be light in this dark world, willing to be more aggressive when led to do so or the occasion truly calls for it.

My wife has led souls to Christ at church altars. And she certainly knows how to lead a soul to Christ outside the church when the scene calls for it. One such situation occurred when my niece's mother-in-law was in the hospital, dying from heart disease. My wife felt led to go talk with her. Though there were others sitting around in the room, Kathy confronted the bed-fast dying sinner with the challenge to prepare for eternity. She prayed the sinner's prayer with my wife and died not long thereafter. But, and this is a big BUT, my wife had heard me on a number of occasions teach how to do the work of an evangelist. If you will but learn the method I teach soon in this book, and if you will ask the Lord for the opportunity (and really WANT an opportunity), you can and will lead souls to Christ!

Meanwhile, you can still be "a bearer of good news" without preaching. Here are several things every Christian can do…

- **Smile a lot.** Don't wait until you feel like smiling. Make yourself smile. If anybody on earth has a good reason to smile it is a child of the living God! By making myself smile at some cashier, I've been asked things like, "You're sure happy today! What are you so happy about?" That question gives me the invitation to give a brief witness for Christ. Or I'll hand them my tract, and say, "Read this and you'll see why." As Ecclesiastes 8:1 says, "A wise man's wisdom makes his face shine." Soul-winners are wise, so manifest that wisdom in a smile.

- **Hand out tracts.** I'll soon give you a few instructions to help you best use a tract to reach the lost.

- **Share your testimony** of how you got saved. Sometimes Paul explained the truth of the Scriptures, and other times he shared how he found Christ. People can argue with you about doctrine, but no one can argue against your personal testimony. You were there! It is the greatest affirmation of the truth of what you believe.

- **Talk about the Lord often in conversations.** Be quick to share what the Lord has done for you lately. Say, "God bless you." Show God's goodness in your life, words, and deeds. "...show others the goodness of God, for he called you out of the darkness into his wonderful light" (1 Peter 2:9 NLT).

I do not want to mislead you. I do not witness or preach to everyone I meet. Even as a God-ordained evangelist, I know God does not require me to bear that heavy of a burden. I wouldn't want to cast a pall of condemnation on you either. Yet, you walk around with the Creator of the Universe dwelling inside of you. You are, like a bolt of lightning, charging with light and power the very atmosphere around you wherever you are. You do not always have to start preaching to people. As St. Francis of Assisi famously said,

"Preach the Gospel at all times. When necessary, use words."

Be aware at all times that the world is watching you and that you are Christ's gospel representative on earth: "Your very lives are a letter that anyone can read by just looking at you" (2 Corinthians 3:2 MSG). People read your face, they read your actions, but when will words be necessary? You can only learn this by experience and/or by being led by the Holy Spirit. Until those times come, you can still always be alert, be real, and be ready.

Light up the room with the Light of the world.

I was in the Southwest Airlines boarding area when my cell phone rang. It was one of my supporters. As a full-time evangelist, I am quite dependent on generous financial supporters to help me concentrate on the ministry. So, I walked over and leaned against a wall where I wouldn't lose my place in line and could hear the boarding call, yet I'd have a little more privacy to talk. I soon discovered I wasn't far enough from others to keep from being overheard. The supporter and I visited on the phone for a while, and then I prayed for her. I got back in my place near the front of the line since Frequent flyers board first.

Behind me in line was a pilot, waiting like me for a seat to fly home. We visited together and talked about airplanes and flying and enjoyed pleasant conversation and banter until it was time to board. I didn't bring up religion in the conversation: I don't ALWAYS do that! I can talk about many topics without feeling guilty for not trying to sneak the gospel on everybody!

One of the ground staff happened to be heading for the plane at the same time as I was. As we walked down the jetway to the plane, he said, "I overheard you praying on the phone. I am a Christian too!" I said, "Praise the Lord brother!" I then wrapped my arm around him as we sauntered together, and I spoke a blessing over him. Walking directly behind us was that pilot. As the three of us entered the plane, I overheard the pilot tell the employee, "He's like a breath of fresh air, isn't he?"

I did not preach. I simply was pleasant, showed interest in a man, prayed for a woman, and spoke a blessing over a Southwest employee. I did nothing noteworthy to be mentioned in church history books. Yet, I was air, life, and light to the world nearby me. Because Christ is within you, you can light up any room! In whatever environment you find yourself strive to be like a...

"Breath of fresh air."

17

THE POWER OF THE GOSPEL

"Then Peter stood up... in a loud voice began to speak to the crowd...'listen to me'...When they heard this, they were deeply troubled and said to Peter and the other apostles, 'What shall we do, Brothers'" (Acts 2:14, 37 GNT)?

I know what many of you are thinking! "Dea, this 'do the work of an evangelist' stuff is easy for you. You ARE an evangelist! You have all the talents to help you: extrovert personality, natural public speaking abilities, a quick wit, and many, many years of experience. I have tried to witness before but just didn't seem to know what to say. Besides I am, to be honest, terrified at the thought!" Well, if you have been thinking thoughts like that while reading this book, I have some good news for you...

Anybody and I do mean ANYBODY can win souls. I have seen proof of that through the years. At a church in Parkrose, Oregon, I taught the mechanics how to step-by-step give a presentation of the gospel with the goal of actually leading someone to Christ. Two days later, a fourth-grade girl came up to me during the evening service and said, "Guess what, Brother Warford?" (Oh, those were the good old days when fellow

Christians referred to each other as brother or sister. It was great when if you had forgotten a name you could simply greet people with, "Oh, Brother, so good to see you! Hi Sister!"). The young girl then told me, "I led one of my friends to Christ at school today!" It's so easy, even kids can win people to Christ!

When I pastored in Lakeview, Oregon, I taught the members principles of soul-winning. A middle-aged woman in the church named Martha Padget was demure, quiet, and reserved. But now she knew how to turn conversations into soul-winning ventures. She visited a young couple, Ron and Charlee Coleman, who were renting a house from her. Martha sat down with them and shared what she had been taught. They both received Christ and began attending our church. Years later, when I came back to town to speak, they both were seated in the audience and still serving the Lord! Subsequently, Ron died of cancer, but he died a Christian. Martha has rewards awaiting her in heaven because she refused to believe that only loud extroverts can win souls!

Perhaps you think you are too old? My mother was in her eighties when she flew with me to spend time together during one of my evangelistic crusades. I marveled as I overheard her sharing the gospel with the man seated next to her on the airplane, especially when he prayed the sinner's prayer with her, while the evangelist just quietly read his book!

At the Anaheim Foursquare Church, Jack Hayford taught the same soul-winning techniques that he taught our freshman class at Bible College. An older woman in the church told me that she had visited with a friend and asked, "Would you mind if I practice something with you that they have been teaching us at my church?" The woman complied with her request.

After the "practice", she dared ask her friend if she would like to receive the Lord? You guessed it, her friend wanted to not just practice but to do it! This older lady again showed the wisdom of learning and then using a proven method of evangelism.

I knew a woman taking a college class. One day, after the class, she started witnessing to her professor. The professor interrupted with, "But what about this?" followed by some intellectual reason to not be a Christian. She replied, "I don't know the answer to that question, but I do know that Jesus loves you." Then he asked, "But what about this other?" She didn't know and told him so, but then added, "But I do know that Jesus loves you." Once more he gave another typical academic rebuttal, to which she said, "I don't know the answer to that, but I do know that Jesus loves you." Tears welled up in the professor's eyes, and he gave his heart to Him!

The simplest gospel presentation on any Christian's lips can prove the words of Paul in Romans 1:16, "I am not ashamed of the gospel of Christ, for IT is the power of God to salvation to everyone who believes." Notice I have highlighted the word "IT." It, that is, "the gospel" is "the power of God" that leads people to salvation. The gospel, not great intellect, not debating skills, not tear-jerking stories. The gospel, of itself, is full of power! I learned this truth graphically when I was still a youth minister at Upland.

Proof of the Gospel's Power

I was invited to a high school graduation party at the home of a teenager who invited someone from our youth group. That night the newly launched "adults" were smoking, drinking, and enjoying liberation from the confines of their high school years. I introduced myself to a teenager, Joe Beckley, who held a beer can in one hand and a cigarillo in the other. Shortly, I began to preach the gospel to him. While I was still speaking, without any suggestion from me, he fell to his knees, in spite of other teenagers milling around us. On his own, he cried out to God for salvation.

Joe rose to his feet, now appearing stone sober. Again, without any suggestion from me, he threw his half-full beer can into the nearby orange grove. Then, he also threw away his cigarillo. After that, he immediately started walking around trying to somehow warn other youth about their need for God. The now just minutes old new convert didn't have an inkling of what he should say. But at least he was saying something, which is more than we can say of many long-term converts! He wasn't making the progress that he hoped for, so we began to talk and soon discovered that we had, not only a mutual friend in Jesus but also a mutual friend in Norm Rush. Discovering that connection, Joe wanted to share the good news of his conversion with Norm.

Joe and I drove together to Norm's home. Norm was one of the heaviest sleepers I have ever known. We could not knock loud enough to awaken him, so we went to the backyard to his bedroom window. Together, we opened it, climbed through the window, turned on the lights, and Norm, still fighting sleep, listened to Joe testify of his newly found faith. I sat amazed that all I had done was confront someone with the gospel, and that gospel, "IT", became "the power" of God resulting in salvation.

I was returning home from a walk one evening. Several townhomes in my track were being fumigated for termites and I noticed that a security guard had been posted nearby to protect the homes from thieves. He was just sitting in his wide-open car trunk doing nothing. It was too perfect an opportunity to witness to not at least approach him, which I did.

I discovered that he had accepted Christ years ago but had done little more about it. We will see in the next chapter that "accepting Christ" means far more than just a one-time convenient prayer. I talked with him at length about what is required of true Christians and the importance of attending church (which he did not do!). Before I left, he talked like he would get back in church. Then, he told me that when I walked up to him and started conversing with him...

"I felt a tingle in my spine!"

"Then the Lord said to Samuel: "Behold, I will do something in Israel at which both ears of everyone who hears it will tingle" (1 Samuel 3:11).

You will be amazed at the inherent power of the gospel! When you put the gospel on your lips, those who hear your words will, at times, respond dramatically. Expect it when you witness, confident in the power of the gospel! Help sinners feel...

The "tingle" of the Holy Spirit convicting them of sin!

18

FOUNDATIONAL TRUTHS FOR EVANGELISM

"...elementary principles of Christ... the foundation of repentance from dead works... of the doctrine of baptisms... and of eternal judgment" (Hebrews 6:1, 2).

We cannot explore all of the "elementary principles" mentioned in Hebrews 6. However, I have selected several that I feel are essential to communicate to the unsaved. Let's study them in order. I will also tell you a story of a flight attendant that I led to Christ which illustrates the truth I convey in this chapter.

Repentance

The noun "repentance" and its verb "repent" are not heard much in today's preaching. Yet they are an "elementary principle" of Christianity! Not only was repentance mentioned first on the list of the above foundational truths, but it was also mentioned first in much biblical preaching:

Christ preached, "Repent, and believe the gospel" (Mark 1:15). Notice He didn't say "just believe!" Later, in Revelation Chapters 2 and 3, He mentioned the word "repent" seven times!

John the Baptist preached "Repent"…"Prove by the way you live that you have repented of your sins and turned to God" (Matt. 3:2, 8 NLT). He didn't just say, "Repeat this prayer after me."

Peter the Apostle preached, "Repent and be baptized" (Acts 2:38). And, "The Lord…is not willing that any should perish but that all should come to repentance" (2 Peter 3:9). The only way not to perish is to repent! "Repent, therefore and be converted, that your sins may be blotted out" (Acts 3:19). How are a sinner's sins blotted out? By just asking for forgiveness and being converted? No, a sinner must "repent."

Paul the Apostle preached repentance, "I preached that they must repent of their sins and turn to God and do the things that would show they had repented" (Acts 26:20 GNT). Paul was the greatest preacher of grace in the Bible, but he did not preach a gospel of grace without repentance!

God Himself commands repentance, "Truly, these times of ignorance God overlooked, but now commands all men everywhere to repent" (Acts 17:30). "All men everywhere" must do something to be saved and what is that something? "Repent."

If the above verses don't convince you that confessing, believing, receiving, praying and such things are not, in themselves, enough in the conversion experience, the Great Commission, Christ's command to the church throughout the ages, should: "…repentance FOR the forgiveness of sins will be preached in His name to all nations" (Luke 24:47 NIV). See that "FOR"? Repentance is a NECESSARY requirement to be forgiven. Thus, a gospel without a clarion "repent" is NOT the gospel at all!

Thank God that in His grace, many have been saved through the centuries without hearing specifically about repentance. The Holy Spirit can do a work in the heart which results in the equivalent of true repentance. Nevertheless, we cannot assume this will happen without preaching repentance. Otherwise, repentance would not have been such a key feature of biblical preaching.

Many stillbirths and many backslidings happen in America. It's estimated that as many as 1 out of 10 who respond to the gospel by praying a sinner's prayer will not follow up on that decision, become a true disciple of Christ, get established in a church, or become a viable representative on earth of the kingdom of God.

Let me share from my journeys one clear example of this truth. Heading toward Albuquerque, New Mexico to preach four services, as usual, I prayed that the Lord would lead someone to sit next to me, someone I could either lead to Christ, minister to them or they could minister to me. Maybe, like, being quiet? The last person on the plane was a flight attendant flying on standby. She sat next to me. I learned that she was 37, had been a flight attendant for a decade, and was not married but had a boyfriend.

Later in the flight, while reading my Bible stretched out on the tray in front of me, I asked her, "Do you study the Bible?' She admitted that she didn't. I asked her where she went to church. She said she went to a non-denominational one, though not regularly.

I further asked her, "If this jet were to crash, are you 100% sure that you would go to heaven?" She said she was. Then, I asked, as the "Evangelism Explosion" study recommends, (see Chapter 19), "If you were to stand before God, and He were to ask you, 'Why should I let you into My heaven?' What would you say?" She said, "I try to live a good, clean life and ask God to forgive me when I sin, etc." She then described an epiphany type of experience she had when she was twenty. Though raised a Catholic, she always felt fear and something amiss when she was in her church.

While visiting a Baptist church, the pastor asked all those who wanted to receive Christ to stand. She said that she was one of maybe 50 who stood that day and prayed a sinner's prayer. That indicated that she was obviously a woman with exposure to Christian truth. Next, I became bold and asked her if she was living with her boyfriend. She admitted she was. I then showed her the verse in Revelation 21:8, "But the...sexually immoral... shall have their part in the lake which burns with fire and brimstone."

I showed her other Scriptures that reveal that we cannot practice sin, must repent, forsake sin, and continue living for Christ. After this, she understood that to "repent" didn't mean to just pray a sinner's prayer, but meant to forsake and then to actually turn away from the practice of sin. Following this foundation of truth, I asked her, "Do you want to go to hell?" She said, "Of course not!" I then asked, "Are you willing to repent of sexual immorality, of living with your boyfriend? And when you get home, will you announce to him that you cannot sleep with him anymore until you are married?" She said she was willing to do that. I then led her in the sinner's prayer.

A confession of sin and of one's need of the Savior of itself will not save a lost soul. There must also be true repentance. Make sure if you ever seek to lead a soul to Christ that they understand this sine qua non of the gospel! Repentance must be heart-motivated especially by turning away from what Hebrews 6:2 calls...

Dead Works

Dead works are self-defined. They include any "work," kind act, or "good deed" which one might rely upon or hope would gain them entrance into heaven. Such things are "dead" in the water, at least when it comes to obtaining eternal life. Probably more people expect their works to get them into heaven than any other misconception.

I have proven this over and over by asking the question, as I have shown in previous chapters, "If you were to die today and God were to ask you, 'Why should I let you into my heaven,' what would you say?" Most people will say something like, "Because I keep the commandments," or " I try to live a good life," or as one sweet teenage girl said, "Because I am really nice." These or similar answers are a dead giveaway that such persons are not saved. "There are people who think they are pure when they are as filthy as they can be" (Proverbs 30:12 GNT). Help these, who are duped by the devil, to clean their "filthy garments" the only way that will make them clean in God's eyes, having, "washed their robes and made them white in the blood of the Lamb" (Revelation 7:14).

That we are not saved by our works is one of the most repeated themes in the New Testament. Thus, when people say such things they prove a great ignorance of the Bible plan of salvation. "My people are destroyed for lack of knowledge" (Hosea 4:6). Don't you think that you have some responsibility to help people who lack this knowledge to attain it?

Baptisms

In our American society water baptism is considered by many THE point of salvation. It is called "baptismal regeneration," the belief that regeneration or salvation does NOT take place until the moment of water baptism. We want to correct that error by pointing confused people to the truth of salvation by grace through faith. Nevertheless, we must still remain true to biblical examples where water baptism was shown to be expected of new believers. Water baptism is very important, or it would not be included in the list of foundational doctrines.

Phillip, the prototype evangelist (our biblical example of how to "do the work of an evangelist"), gave the Ethiopian Eunuch the gospel. Phillip surely must have emphasized baptism in that message since his new convert did not wait for the next monthly church baptismal service. No! As they passed a pool of water in Acts 8:36, the Eunuch said, "See, here is water. What hinders me from being baptized?"

After Saul met Christ on the Damascus road, he was led to the house of Ananias who told Paul, "…why are you waiting? Arise and be baptized, and wash away your sins [metaphorically], calling on the name of the Lord" (Acts 22:16). After his experience, Paul must have been convinced of the importance of water baptism. He proved it in his gospel presentation to the Philippian jailor, because though it was past midnight, they didn't even wait for daybreak! "And immediately he and all his family were baptized" (Acts 16:33).

It would be hard to explain away Mark 16:16, "He who believes and is baptized will be saved." Jesus was not saying that a person is only half-saved until he is baptized, then he receives the other half of his salvation as he comes out of the water.

We know this for a fact because of the thief on the cross. When the thief cried, "Lord, remember me when You come into Your kingdom", Jesus did not reply, "Oh, I'm so sorry. It's too late because you can't be baptized on that cross." Rather, Jesus told him, "Today you will be with me in Paradise" (Luke 23:42, 3).

The thief was saved without being baptized. If there is one exception to a rule, there can be many, many more exceptions. Water baptism never has and never will save a lost soul. It is, however, one first and very important step we take toward the ongoing "good works" to which we all are destined: "God has made us what we are. He has created us in Christ

Jesus to live lives filled with good works that he has prepared for us to do" (Eph. 2:10 GW).

How then do I harmonize a gospel of grace by faith with the necessity of water baptism? That is a simple question to answer…

Saved people get baptized!

Even Jesus was baptized in water! Water baptism is an outward sign of an inward work. It is a symbolic act of sins being washed away. The act also shows we fully embrace the gospel, not just parts we like about it, but in its entirety. As John the Baptist warned,

"Repent"…"Prove by the way you live that you have repented of your sins and turned to God" (Matt. 3:2, 8 NLT).

If a sinner truly turns to the Lord, then he will follow the Savior into the waters of baptism, if not immediately, eventually. To leave a new convert with the impression that all he had to do was pray a little prayer and "voila," is a travesty of the truth! If new converts won't make a splash in a church baptismal tank for their faith, they will hardly make a splash as a Christian out in the world!

Because of so much confusion, child baptisms, sprinklings, baptism for unsaved people, etc., most pastors and evangelists do not bring up the subject until there is some evidence of a true conversion. John the Baptist refused to baptize Pharisees who came to be baptized because he knew it was just some religious work to them and they had not had a true conversion. Thus, he told them, "Do those things that prove you have turned to God and have changed the way you think and act" (Matthew 3:8 GW).

Once a new convert starts attending church and shows a renewed heart and teachable spirit, they will be amenable to water baptism. We must however not leave it up to the whim of new believers as to when or if they ever get baptized. Our Great Commission is to...

"Go therefore and make disciples of all the nations, baptizing them in the name of the Father and of the Son and of the Holy Spirit, teaching them to observe all things that I have commanded you (Matthew 28:19, 10).

Teaching them the importance of water baptism and then actually baptizing them is an integral aspect of discipling any new convert.

Eternal Judgment

Jesus preached more about hell than He did heaven. Why? Do you think it could be because hell is so horrible that it was in the heart of the Savior to help people escape it? This is in my heart. I think about hell a lot. In a church in Arizona, from the pulpit, I asked the congregation the following question:

"If Jesus were to give you the opportunity to visit heaven for five minutes to see what it is like or to visit hell for five minutes, which offer would you accept? How many of you would rather go to heaven for five minutes, raise your hands?"

Virtually every hand went up.

Then I asked, "How many of you would rather go to hell for five minutes, raise your hands?"

I raised my hand. I was the only one in that church who raised his hand to visit hell. Why would I want to visit hell? I figure if I could ever experience the darkness, the pain, the cries of agony, maybe when I came back to earth I would more readily witness. I would never again yield to fear, pride, embarrassment, or selfishness. I would help many more to escape eternal punishment.

That probably is not going to happen to me or you. But, we don't need to actually see hell. "We walk by faith and not by sight" (2 Corinthians 5:7). The doctrine of hell is one of the most clearly spelled out biblical doctrines of all. Following is a list of many descriptions of hell. Let the Lord pierce your heart even deeper than it may already be in fulfillment of Ecclesiastes 3:11,

> "He has put eternity in their hearts."

Jesus described hell like this: "danger of hell fire" and "your whole body...cast into hell" (Matthew 5:22, 29), "cut down and thrown into the fire" (7:19), "cast out into outer darkness: there shall be weeping and gnashing of teeth" (8:12), "destroy both soul and body in hell" (10:28), "cast them into a furnace of fire" (13:42), "cast into everlasting fire" (18:8), "the damnation of hell" (Matthew 23:33), "the fire that shall never be quenched" (Mark 9:44 NKJV), and, "shall be beaten with many stripes" (Luke 12:47).

Paul the Apostle wrote similarly awful things about hell: "the day of wrath" and "indignation and wrath...and anguish" (Romans 2:5, 8), "the terror of the Lord" (2 Corinthians 5:11), "punished with everlasting destruction from the presence of the Lord" (2 Thessalonians 2:9), "fiery indignation which shall devour" (Hebrews 10:27).

Jude describes very descriptive aspects of hell: "the vengeance of eternal fire" and "the blackness of darkness forever" (Jude 7, 13).

John the Revelator surely resolves any doubts about the subject: "They shall be tormented with fire and brimstone… the smoke of their torment ascends up forever and ever" (Revelation 14:10, 11), "A lake of fire burning with brimstone" (19:20), "they will be tormented day and night forever and ever" (20:10).

Hell is hot! Hell is horrible! And hell is forever and ever! Imagine for just a moment a friend, neighbor or family member experiencing the above horrors. If that thought, and a very real one at that, alone does not motivate you to witness, then there is certainly nothing I could possibly write to change that.

You are likely one of those who would raise your hand asking for a five-minute visit to heaven. May I urge you to now raise your hand to the Lord and ask Him for a personal, clearer revelation of how awful hell surely is? When you are fully convinced of the reality of a literal, eternal, and dreadful hell, that truth will motivate you to witness as perhaps nothing else can.

Will you give five minutes of your time today, in prayer, in witnessing, to help but one sinner escape…

5 trillion years in hell!

19

ASKING THE RIGHT QUESTIONS

"Be as cunning as a snake, inoffensive as a dove"
(Matthew 10:16 MSG).

Because sinners rarely, if ever, start a conversation about the Bible or the Lord, you must take the initiative. I've conversed with many people through the years and listened to them talk about themselves, sometimes by the hour, without them mentioning spiritual things one time!

While flying from Denver to Ontario, a two-hour flight, I sat next to a man who loved to talk. I thought to myself, "I am going to see how long this guy will talk." From the moment we took off until the moment we landed, two hours later, except for a few very brief comments from me, he talked incessantly. I determined I would never do that again!

People love to talk about themselves. I have been amazed at how people joyfully share their personal monologues, usually without once showing an interest in mine. Thus, you must learn to be "cunning as a snake" and as "inoffensive as a dove" to maneuver a conversation around other subjects and into a soul-winning opportunity. To do this, you easily, politely, and pleasantly ask the right questions.

The "Encounter Method"

The "Encounter Method," which I learned as a 17-year-old, suggests three questions which I used often during my earlier years of personal evangelism. These questions cunningly move the conversation towards a presentation of the gospel. They are inoffensive also to most people.

The questions are easy to memorize as well (This is used by permission from the surviving daughter of the author of the book, *Soul-Winning Made Easy*, by C.S. Lovett, now out of print, but you can buy a used copy on Amazon.com inexpensively).

1. "Are you interested in spiritual things?" Regardless of how they answer, you move to the next question.

2. "Have you ever thought about becoming a Christian?" Their answer to the first few questions usually tells you a lot about their spiritual life. Regardless of how they answer, you then move to the next question.

3. "If someone were to ask you, 'What is a Christian?' what would you say?" If they say, "Hallelujah! A Christian is washed in the blood of the Lamb, a committed follower of Jesus Christ, and looking forward to heaven!" then they probably are already saved! But usually, they will say something like "a Christian believes in God, keeps the commandments, lives a good life, etc." indicative that they are very likely NOT a Christian.

C.S. Lovett suggests that to each wrong answer you reply, "Yes, that's true. A Christian tries to DO all those things, but just what IS he? He is different from all others. He has something no one else has...can you think what that might be?" Many give up at this point, thus providing you with a great opening to answer your own question.

If they should answer, "It is someone who has accepted Christ," you can ask, "Have you done that?" If they say they have, then ask them, "Please, tell me about your experience and how it changed your life." C.S. Lovett calls this "the X-ray approach." Their answer really helps you to discern if they are walking with the Lord or not. If you are unsatisfied that they know the Lord, you can say, "Yes, that indeed is part of it alright, but being a true Christian is even more than that."

Whatever definitions of a Christian may have been offered by the person, if you still in your heart question their spiritual health, then you ask them one more question.

4. "If it's alright with you, I'd like to read you four verses of Scriptures and explain them to you, then you'll know what a Christian is. That would be okay, wouldn't it?" If they say yes, you have carte blanche to preach the gospel to them. You would be surprised how many people are willing to let you share some Bible verses with them. If they are not interested, you can be "cunning" and "inoffensive" by pleasantly closing the conversation by smiling and saying, "Perhaps some other time. It's just that learning what a Christian is and being a true Christian has so changed my life for the good. Thanks for listening to me though."

If the person is willing to have you share with them, you either have the four Scriptures memorized, or marked with scotch-tape tabs on a pocket New Testament so that you can read them and use them as a platform from which you preach the truth. The "Encounter Method" suggests you use Romans 3:23, 6:23, John 1:12 and Revelation 3:20 to explain the gospel. I have led many souls to Christ using those verses of Scripture. However, when I was pastoring back in the 1980s, I discovered a book that taught a plan that I preferred and began using instead of the Encounter Method.

The "Evangelism Explosion" Method

The book *Evangelism Explosion* written by the late Dr. James Kennedy has what, in my opinion, are even better questions to turn a conversation around to a soul-winning opportunity. (The following is used by permission of Tyndale House Publishers. I have added some things that I've discovered after decades of using this approach that makes the conversation move more smoothly).

Start out with a pleasant conversation about anything, from which you can then "cunningly" and "inoffensively" bring up the subject of spiritual things. Dr. Kennedy suggests two basic questions from which you continue to guide the conversation. I'll usually preface the first question by saying, "I have an interesting question I like to ask people to see what their answer is…"

1. "Have you come to the place in your spiritual life where you know for certain that if you were to die today you would go to heaven?" Most people will say something like, "No" or "I think so" or "No one can know that." Even if they say, "Oh, yes I would", you still ask the second question.

2. "Suppose you were to die today and stand before God and He were to say to you, 'Why should I let you into My heaven?' What would you say?"

Most will say such things as, "because I live a good life," "because I believe in God," or even "I'm not sure there is life after death." Regardless of what they say, you can respond, "I discovered something wonderful. I discovered it was possible to know for sure! I even discovered that was the reason the Bible was written. The Scripture says, 'These things I have written unto you… that you may know that you have eternal life" (1 John 5:13). Then, you immediately follow up with the third question.

3. "May I share my brief testimony of how I came to the assurance that I am going to heaven and share some Scriptures that show the only way to really be sure of going to heaven?"

If they say, "no," just pleasantly close the conversation as explained above. You have planted a seed and given them something to think about. But if they say, "yes," you have declared approval to preach the gospel! I strongly recommend you buy *Evangelism Explosion* by James Kennedy, Tyndale, 1996, for further study. It is an outstanding guide for any serious soul-winner.

Evangelist Ray Comfort's Method

While I was pastoring in Hawaiian Gardens, I had lunch one day with Ray Comfort, an evangelist who wrote the book, *Hell's Best Kept Secret*. Ray also helped equip me to better "Do the work of an evangelist." The questions God gave Ray to ask proved to be some of the most useful of all questions, and I have asked them often. His book, *The School of Biblical Evangelism*, co-written with born-again actor Kirk Cameron, with its 768 pages, reads like an Encyclopedia of Soul-Winning. Evangelist Ray Comfort may be the greatest personal evangelist alive in America today. Go to his website to receive inspirational help, watch his training videos and some of his well-made movies, and buy his books and tracts. His website is www.livingwaters.com.

Ray's unique method of evangelism is to use the 10 Commandments, contained in the Law, as a tool to dig deeply into the heart of a sinner, revealing their worthiness of judgment from God. Paul wrote, "I would not have known sin except through the law. For I would not have known covetousness unless the law had said, 'You shall not covet'" (Romans 7:7). Therefore, by using the law, you can show self-righteous sinners that they are actually guilty before God. I have permission from Ray's office to use some of his techniques from his books. I have paraphrased and gleaned from his books the suggested approach below. Here might be a typical question and answer segment, with further comments following their answers, of a conversation about the Law after you have "cunningly" gained one's listening ear.

Q: "Do you feel that you know God?"

A: "Yes, I have been a Christian all my life."

Q: "Are you aware that the Bible says, 'If someone claims, I know God,' but doesn't obey God's commandments, that person is a liar and is not living in the truth' (1 John 2:4 NLT)?"

A: "Hadn't read that verse before."

Q: "Do you keep His commandments."

A: "Yes, I think so."

Q: "Here's a little self-evaluation quiz I give people about the 10 Commandments. Do you always put God first in your life?"

A; "No, probably not."

Q: The very first commandment says, "Thou shalt have no other gods before me" (Exodus 20:3 KJV). To put anything, person, or activity before God is a form of idolatry. So, do you think maybe at times you are guilty of idolatry?"

A: "Maybe".

Q: "The 3rd commandment is, "Thou shalt not take the name of the Lord your God in vain; for the Lord will not hold him guiltless that taketh His Name in vain" (Exodus 20:7 KJV). Have you ever used God's Name in vain?"

A: "Sure, sometimes when I get mad."

Q: "Did you know that act means you're guilty of blasphemy and the Bible says, "Your enemies take Your name in vain" (Psalm 138:20)? Do you want to be a blasphemer and an enemy of God?"

A: "Of course not."

Q: "The 7th commandment says, "Thou shalt not commit adultery" (Exodus 20:13). Have you ever lusted after someone of the opposite sex?"

A: "Lots of times."

Q: "Jesus said, 'Whoever looks at a woman to lust for her has already committed adultery with her in his heart'" (Matthew 5:28). The Bible also warns that "neither fornicators...nor adulterers...will inherit the kingdom of God" (1 Corinthians 6:19, 20). So, do you want to be an adulterer in God's eyes and miss out on eternal life?

A: Silence

Q: "The 8th commandment is "Thou shalt not steal" (Exodus 10:15 KJV). Have you ever stolen anything?"

A: "When I was younger, maybe."

Q: "If you only stole once that still makes you a thief in God's eyes, doesn't it?"

A: "I guess."

Q: "The 9th commandment is "Thou shalt not bear false witness" (Exodus 20:16). Have you ever told a lie in your whole life?"

A: "Who hasn't?"

Q: "Did you know the book of Revelation says, "All liars shall have their part in the lake which burns with fire and brimstone, which is the second death" (Revelation 21:8)?" Do you want to spend eternity in a lake of fire?

A: "What do you think?"

Then you wrap it all up with, "I really appreciate your honesty. We all have broken God's laws and are sinners in the eyes of a Holy God. By your own admission, you are an idolater, an adulterer, a blasphemer, a thief, and a liar (or just list any commandments they confessed to breaking).

"Whoever breaks one commandment is guilty of breaking them all" (James 2:10 GNT). "According to God's Word, you are guilty before God, as we all are. You need a Savior. Let me briefly explain how to know you are forgiven of all those past sins." Then, if they will allow you to do so, proceed in sharing the gospel.

Ask the right questions

See the wisdom of using leading questions in personal evangelism? Any of the above methods could serve you well. Ask the Lord which line of questioning you should memorize to use in the future. You really can guide any conversation with questions.

One of the simplest and easiest ways to get a conversation going the direction you want it to go is to say something about your church, then ask, "Do you go to church anywhere?" Or as Ray Comfort suggests, "Do you know of any good churches around here?" Whatever their answer, continue your line of questioning further, using any above approach you prefer.

Philip the evangelist started a soul-winning encounter with a question. The Lord had already arranged a perfect situation for the soul-winner. A Eunuch "just happened" to be reading the Old Testament. Philip asked him, "Do you understand what you are reading" (Acts 8:30)? I used that question in door to door ministry when I was planting a church in Bellingham, Washington. It's another great question you can use. Try it…

"Do you understand the Bible?"

The Lord will lead you, like He did with Philip, and also arrange soul-winning encounters for you when you prepare yourself ahead of time with wise questions.

Now you know the questions,

so let's study the right answers…

20

"DEA'S DETOUR": AN EVANGELISTIC TECHNIQUE

"Then Philip *opened his mouth*, and beginning at this Scripture, preached Jesus to him. Now as they went down the road, they came to some water. And the eunuch said, "See, here is water. What hinders me from being baptized'" (Acts 8:35-36)?

Note those three words: "opened his mouth." That's the very first step to any soul-winning encounter: "OPEN YOUR MOUTH!" I know, you're thinking, easy to say, but not so easy to do. Maybe, but just remember that preaching the gospel instead of remaining frozen with fear or doubt is but one more fulfillment of the truth, "We walk by faith and not by sight" (2 Timothy 5:7).

In preparing His disciples for times of persecution and being tried in court for their faith, Jesus assured them, "When you are arrested, don't worry about how to respond or what to say. God will give you the right words at the right time" (Matthew 10:19 NLT). If you can trust Him to give you the right words to say when your life is at stake, then don't you think you can trust the Lord to give you the right words to say when someone else's eternal life is at stake?

God can use your open mouth anytime and at any place to witness for Him. Still, my soul-winning journey began only after I learned and memorized, verbatim, a specific plan from start to finish. Though that plan has evolved through the years because of the many other things I have read and experienced, I am still convinced that you will be most effective and have the most confidence beginning your own soul-winning journey if you know exactly what you intend to say from beginning to end.

To help you do this, in this chapter, I present the ideas that I often use when I witness for Christ. To differentiate it from other plans, I'll refer to it as, "Dea's Detour," since that is what this evangelist is trying to do: turn people away from the "way that leads to death" and to take the gospel detour (Proverbs 14:12).

"Dea's Detour" is based on my tract on the last pages of this book. The advantage of this is so that you will have one proven gospel presentation, written in an easily referenced form in the tract. You could even just read the tract to someone or at least use it as a reminder of each point. If you aren't good at memorization, you could always use the old standby and proven method called, "The Romans Road." All you need is a pocket New Testament which has each verse colorfully marked ahead of time, unless you want to memorize all the verses. Then the Word does much of the preaching for you, and you give a brief explanation of each verse.

The Romans Road

Romans 3:10, 3:23, 6:23 (Share about the lostness of mankind)

Romans 5:8 (Christ is God's solution for man's dilemma)

Romans 10:9-10; 10:13 (The sinner's required response)

Romans 5:1-2; 8:1 (The results new believers can expect)

This is a simplified method. I also recommend adding a few verses about repentance and baptism to the above, but you can always fill in the gaps as you feel needed.

Although you could use any of the questions from the previous chapter before you share this gospel presentation, I have included the question asked in my tract and the question I have used often to open the door to preaching the gospel. Are you ready to learn the single most important thing in this book? May God give you a clear mind and the wisdom of a soul-winner (Proverbs 11:30) as you imbed this message in your heart. Ready or not, here it comes…

Dea's Detour

After at least a brief period of conversation and after you have skillfully maneuvered the trivia and banter towards the spiritual realm, you take control of the direction of your talk with the following line of questioning:

Q: "There is an interesting question I like to challenge people with. Let me ask you, 'Where were you born'?"

A: "Timbuktu"

Q: "When were you born, not the year, but month and day?"

A: "June 27."

Q: "OK. You know where and when you were born on planet earth. Now, here is an even more important question, 'Where and when were you born again?'"

A: "I don't know?"

If they answer with these or similar words, you can immediately transition to the "official" gospel presentation below. However, there are a few other answers you'll commonly receive. When that happens, here are suggestions of how to use their answer to determine the best further action.

A: "I became a born-again Christian about 10 years ago at the Grace Church in Cleveland where I now sometimes attend."

This response gives good evidence that they are indeed already a true follower of Christ. If you discern this, enjoy the Christian fellowship. But if you still have doubts, and just to make sure, I suggest you say the following:

"Wonderful! Oh, let me tell you about my born-again experience." Then testify to every change the new birth brought to your life. Afterward, you ask them to share how being born again changed their life. By their lack of an answer, you have evidence that they are not born again and you will know to say, "Let me share with you what I learned about being born again that clarified the meaning of the experience in my mind." You then immediately begin the gospel presentation below.

Another common answer is...

A: "When I was baptized in the Catholic Church as a baby."

You might respond, "Oh, good. Weren't you blessed to have parents who wanted you to be a Christian? But, according to the Bible, that is not quite enough to be born-again. Let me share with you what I learned about being born again that clarified the meaning of the experience in my mind." You then share your testimony and begin the gospel presentation below.

As you study "Dea's Detour" you will notice that I say additional things and use additional Scriptures which are not in my tract. A tract is just the basic bones of important aspects of the gospel and cannot, in itself, adequately deal with every important doctrinal truth in just a few small pages. Only through conversation can you determine which areas of the gospel need to be stressed or spelled out for each individual.

Below is a fully developed gospel presentation. I say many of these things when I share the gospel. Glean things from it you might also want to say.

The Gospel Presentation

Jesus said there is only one way to get into heaven, "Unless a man is born again, he shall not see the kingdom of God" (John 3:3). If you know where and when you were born, but aren't 100% sure you were ever born again, the Bible shows you how.

Being born again is like the birth of a baby: one day, in a dark womb, the next day, living in the light! "He has called you out of darkness and into His marvelous light" (Romans 3:23). God is urging you to escape what Christ called "outer darkness" or hell.

Jesus talked more about hell than heaven and described it in the worst possible terminology. He said there is, "weeping and gnashing of teeth" (Matthew 8:12). He called it an everlasting fire. I don't want to go to such a place, do you?

Did you know that there is a book in heaven called the Book of Life? On the judgment day, when you stand before God, that book will be opened to see if your name is in it, and the Bible says, "Whoever was not written in the Book of Life was cast into the lake of fire" (Revelation 20:15). Look what is at stake here!

A newborn is given a birth-certificate. Similarly, if you are born again, your name is written in the Book of Life. Either hell or heaven is everyone's destiny. Becoming a born-again Christian is the ONLY WAY to avoid hell and experience eternal light and eternal life. So, is your name written in the Book of Life? If you are in doubt, just make sure you have become a born-again Christian.

How then is a person born again? First, you must repent of your sins. Jesus said, "Unless you repent you will...perish" (Luke 13:3). Repent means to turn away from any habitual, chronic, willful sins and to dedicate yourself to overcoming such sins and to bringing your life in line with Christ's teachings as recorded in the Bible. You will be judged, not by what your church or my church might believe. We both will be judged by the Bible. "The word that I have spoken... will judge him in the last day" (John 12:48). That's why you must not depend on personal beliefs.

God's Word says you're a sinner, "All have sinned and fall short of the glory (presence) of God" (Romans 3:23). You cannot earn the privilege of living in His eternal presence. "He saved us, not because we did the right things, but...by a new birth" (Titus 3:5). Do you think you're good enough in God's eyes? Think again! "There is no one who does good, no, not one" (Romans 3:12).

Do you think that you have a good heart? Think again! "The heart is deceitful above all things and desperately wicked" (Jeremiah 17:9). Your heart may be okay in your eyes, but God sees a lifetime of anger, pride, hatred, jealousy or lust: and all these are "desperately wicked" to Him! Because of these sins, you'll one day face a payday. "The wages of sin is (eternal) death" (Romans 6:23). Not just you and me, but God said, "the entire world is guilty before God" (Romans 3:19 NLT).

All the good deeds you may have done in the past can never compensate, in God's eyes, for your past sins. Imagine a murderer standing before a judge, found guilty. The judge asks him, do you have anything to say before I pronounce your sentence? To which the defendant says, "All my life I did a lot of good things: paid my taxes, was a Boy Scout leader, food-bank volunteer, and obeyed all the other laws. So, couldn't you, on that basis, set me free?"

Of course not! A just judge would still have to give the criminal life in prison. No matter how well you have obeyed God's laws, it is not enough in God's eyes to get you into heaven. You need a Savior. "No one is made right with God by obeying the law. It is by believing in Jesus Christ" (Galatians 2:16 NIRV).

Jesus said, "He who believes and is baptized will be saved" (Mark 16:16). I advise you to bring up the subject of water baptism at this juncture of your witness. By simply quoting this verse, you have planted this important water baptism seed. If they begin questioning you about it, you can either deal with it using some of my suggestions in chapter 18. Or, you can simply avoid something contentious that the devil might use to hinder their decision.

If they get hung up for any reason concerning water baptism, I suggest you simply say…

"You can resolve those questions between you and God later." But, you still must be born again! Then continue…

Jesus invites you personally. He said, "Come to me" (Matthew 11:28). Once you come to Jesus and "repent and believe the gospel" (Mark 1:15), He will receive you and forgive you of all sins. "If we confess our sins, He is faithful to forgive us and to cleanse us from all unrighteousness" (1 John 1:9). Humbly confess your sinfulness and call on Him to save you, "Everyone who calls on the name of the Lord will be saved" (Romans 10:13).

If you were swimming in the ocean and a rip-tide began pulling you out to sea and exhausted, you began to drown, but suddenly saw a lifeguard walking on the shore, what would you say to the lifeguard? "I'm drowning. Save me!" You are drowning in sin but Jesus is ready to hear your prayers for help and save you from hell. Here is His invitation, "Behold, I stand at the door and knock. If anyone hears My voice and opens the door, I will come in to him" (Revelation 3:20).

Jesus is knocking at the door of your heart. He wants to come into your life. He wants to forgive you of every sin you have ever committed. He wants to make you a born-again Christian. He wants to write your name in the book of life. However, the decision is up to you. Do you admit that you are a sinner and in need of a Savior? Do you want to go to heaven instead of hell? Are you willing to become a born-again Christian, since that is the only way to have eternal life? If they respond "yes" to such questions, then ask them if they are willing to pray with you now. If so...

Let's pray right now. Jesus is here, ready to come into your life. Just bow your head and repeat this prayer after me (Lead them slowly, phrase by phrase). "Dear Lord Jesus. I admit I am a sinner. I repent of my sins. Please forgive me. I invite you to come into my heart. Make me a born-again Christian. Write my name in the book of life, so that I can go to heaven instead of hell. I'll go to church, read the Bible, fight sin, fight Satan, and by the grace of God, I'll live for you, for the rest of my life. So help me God."

If they pray that prayer, then you would follow-up as we show you in the next chapter. If they indicate that they are not ready to ask Jesus to come into their heart, ask them "Why not?" By their answer, you will know how to best continue the conversation. Do they understand the gospel and need further clarification? Do they feel they need some time to consider it further? Or are they categorically rejecting Christ as their Savior?

Respond: "I appreciate your honesty. I wouldn't want you to do anything you weren't serious about. But remember, Jesus said He stood at the door of your heart and wanted to come in. If you won't let Him come in, you are saying 'No' to the only person in the universe who can save you. Until you receive Christ into your life, you cannot be a born-again Christian and will not make heaven your eternal home. Think about that, and I certainly hope you don't put that decision off until it is too late. When you die or Christ returns, it will be too late then! I will be praying for you. Please, though, do let me know if you ever change your mind and I can help you in any way I can. I truly care!" Then change the conversation, pleasantly, to another subject.

"Dea's Detour" is just one of many, many ways to present the gospel. Many of the verses and ideas I shared with you in this chapter have worked for me through the years in my own witness. Give it a chance to work for you too! You are not ready yet, however. You must familiarize yourself first with how to follow-up with new converts.

You made it thus far reading this book. Keep with it a little longer. The next chapter is almost as important as this one!

**Tell sinners the only Detour
that can lead them out of hell!**

21

FOLLOW-UP FOR NEW CONVERTS

"When anyone hears the word of the kingdom, and does not understand it, then the wicked one comes and snatches away what was sown in his heart" (Matthew 13:19).

New converts must understand the gospel, or as Jesus warned, the devil can come and literally "snatch away" what has happened in their heart. This is why what soul-winners call, "follow-up" is so important. Born again people have experienced a new birth. But just as a new-born baby cannot live on its own without the help of others, so any new believer in Christ must have the help of their fellow Christians who "follow-up" on their new family member.

The first thing you will want to do after a prayer of repentance is to

Lead them to an assurance of salvation.

Immediately after leading a sinner in a prayer or repentance, review the verses you have used in convincing them to get right with the Lord. I recommend asking the following questions and I show their typical answer.

Q: "Did you mean that prayer?"

A: "Yes, I did!"

Q: "Jesus said, 'I stand at the door and knock. If anyone hears My voice and opens the door, I will come in to him.' Did you open the door of your heart to Christ and ask him to come in?"

A: "Yes."

Q: "Then where is Christ now?" (Point at their heart).

A: "He is in my heart."

Q: "I am so happy for you. The Bible says, 'whoever will call on the name of the Lord will be saved.' Did you call on the Lord and ask Him to save you today?"

A: "Yes."

Q: "So if God promised that 'whoever will call on the name of the Lord will be saved' and you called on Him asking Him to save you, what did He do for you today?"

A; "He saved me."

Q: "Yes! He saved you from the penalty of your sins, from Satan, and an eternity in hell. And now is your name written in the book of life?"

A: "Yes, it must be."

Q: That means you will be let into heaven at the judgment. So far, you have done those things that the Bible says are necessary to be born again. So, are you now a born-again Christian?"

A: "Yes!"

Q: "And if you were to die in your sleep tonight, would you go to heaven or hell?"

A: "Heaven."

So, you have completed the gospel, led them to the Savior, and helped them to understand the basis for the assurance that they are saved, born again and on their way to heaven. However, you are not done yet!

They now must follow Christ.

Explain to them, Jesus said, "follow me" (John 8:12). When you're born again, you show your faith and sincerity to follow Christ by the changes you now make in your life. "If anyone is in Christ, he is a new(born) creation. Old things are passed away. All things are new" (2 Corinthians 5:17). "Old things" (like sins) must be put behind you to concentrate on the "new!" Satan is going to try to steer you away from serving Christ. There are some simple and proven steps to help you to continue with the Lord.

Jesus warned, "But the gate to life is narrow and the way that leads to it is hard" (Matthew 7:14). There is a biblically established pattern for followers of Christ. A few of these ways may be hard for you. Nevertheless, every Christian must change his ways. That is what repentance is all about.

They need to get established in a good home church.

Jesus said, "For where two or three gather together as my followers, I am there among them" (Matthew 18:20). Tell them that Jesus goes to church every Sunday! As a follower of Him, you should too! Satan will tempt you with family, friends, sports, television, etc. "The family of God is the church of the living God. It is the pillar and foundation of the truth" (1 Timothy 3:15 NIRV). The foundation for all truth is the church, and it's your family now.

"Let us not give up the habit of meeting together, as some are doing. Instead, let us encourage one another all the more, since you see that the Day of the Lord is coming nearer (Hebrews 10:25 GNT). Regular church attendance is one habit you must develop to be ready for Christ's return.

Every situation is different, but here is how I recommend you deal with new converts. If they are Catholic, I will often say, "You went to the Catholic Church all these years, yet hadn't learned how to be born again. You might want to prayerfully consider trying another church that can help you find further guidance." The same would be true of any other church if they had been attending there without coming to know the Lord.

If they don't attend church but live in your town, then you want to do your best to get them to at least visit your church. Tell them good things about your church and ask them if they wouldn't mind coming to church with you for the next service. Offer to give them a ride. If they live elsewhere, offer to help them locate a good church by doing an internet search and then get back to them soon with suggestions of evangelical churches near their home.

The Bible

Ask them if they own a modern, easy to read translation. Many only have a King James Bible, which is written in Old English and is difficult for the best readers to understand. Suggest your favorite translation. If they don't own one yet, tell them they can get one at any Christian bookstore or even at Walmart. Or buy them one as a gift, which also allows you an excuse to visit in their home to give it to them and to offer some more spiritual guidance.

Suggest they start reading in the New Testament every day. If you don't, they will probably start in the book of Genesis and by the time they get to Leviticus or Numbers they will give up in frustration. Later they can learn the value of books like the Psalms, Proverbs and eventually study the entire Old Testament.

Daily Prayer

Explain to them what prayer is. Describe your personal devotional life and how it helps you get through the day. Tell them the importance of a prayer closet and a regular time to go there. I will usually also tell a new convert, "Now that you are born again, that doesn't mean you will never sin again. But it means that you have a means of forgiveness now. "But if we confess our sins to him, he is faithful and just to forgive us our sins and to cleanse us from all" (1 John 1:9 NLT).

Warn them that if they yield to some temptation or revert to some long-term bad-habit, that Satan may tell them,

"You're not really born again. Look what you did again. Forget about this Christian stuff.'"

But He is a liar. The Lord said He would forgive you. Confess your sin and believe you are forgiven. Then seek His help to overcome that sin through prayer and Bible reading or counselling with a fellow believer. (Remember when my cousin David told me, "I thought you got saved at camp?" It is one of the devil's oldest trick in his book to dissuade new believers). There is still much more you can do...

Give them a book.

I told the story earlier of how just a small booklet about what it means to follow Christ became the catalyst which transformed a new convert, Cheryl Rackley's life. I highly recommend you give a new believer at least a booklet as a resource for them to continue on their pursuit of God. I plan to write one myself which should be made available for purchase in the next edition of this book. Until then, I recommend the blue colored booklet, "Now What? A guidebook for New Christians," by Ralph W. Harris, which you can purchase inexpensively at www.myhealthychurch.com. The website also carries new convert books for youth and for children.

Encourage them to witness for Christ.

Help them to see how important it is that they boldly testify of their faith. Jesus said, "All those who stand before others and say they believe in me, I will say before my Father in heaven that they belong to me" (Matthew 10:32). He also said, "If people are ashamed of me and my teaching, then the Son of Man will be ashamed of them when he comes" (Luke 9:26 NCV). If you are too proud to tell people that you are a believer and follower of Christ, then the Lord will be ashamed of you when He comes.

Say to the new believer,

"Today, if I had been ashamed to share my faith with you, you would still not be born again. Think about it! You have family and friends who aren't yet born again. You don't want them to go to hell, do you? Of course not! So, God's plan is for every Christian to do his best to win those he knows to Christ. When you get home, begin by telling your family what happened to you and share with them, as I did with you, how a person is born again."

As they are sincerely paying attention now, add this again…

Water Baptism by Immersion

As I suggested earlier, you don't need to get into the subject of water baptism until they have started attending church. When you see evidence of their new birth, you can then review with your new convert the importance of this most basic act of obedience.

Advise them that a baptismal service is an ideal time to invite friends and family to witness this occasion. The public demonstration of their new-found faith by baptism is one powerful way to become a witness for Christ. In addition, friends and family will likely want to come just to honor them. When they are in the service, some may hear the gospel for the first time during the pastor's sermon and get saved.

Finally, be sure to get at least their email address. You will want to send them encouragement and invitations to church, Bible studies or whatever your relationship with them allows. New converts will often give me their E-mail address to receive E-mail teachings I send out. If they live near you, get their physical address and even phone number if you can!

Be aggressive in your follow-up! If you aren't, I guarantee the devil will!

What about backsliders?

I was on another jet, seated next to a dentist. We had barely taken off when he ordered three shots of hard liquor and two beers. The five glasses were spread out on the seat-back table in front of him. Soon, I was sharing with him my testimony and the gospel. When I asked him if he had been born again, he said he hadn't. After more conversation, he exclaimed, "Oh, I forgot! I was born again when I was nine, and my Baptist preacher uncle prayed with me. He soon added after that, "I don't believe in talking politics or religion."

Here's a theological question. Was this dentist saved and on his way to heaven because he had accepted Christ as a nine-year-old, even though he now was probably an alcoholic who didn't believe in talking religion and had all but forgotten that he had been born again? There are two schools of thought about this.

First is the belief that once people are saved and born again, they will remain saved for the rest of their life. They may fall out of fellowship with the Lord and the church, but they remain saved by grace through faith. This is often referred to as the doctrine of "eternal security."

Second is the belief that saved Christians are indeed saved by grace through faith. Still, they are given a free-will, which God will never violate, and thus, they are responsible to maintain their relationship with a Holy God. They can rebel against God, as Satan did, and depart from the path of eternal life. Their salvation can be lost through unbelief or willful, continual, habitual sin, and disobedience to the gospel. As you probably have already discerned, I am of this theological persuasion.

Every believer is indeed "eternally secure," but there is a condition to maintain that security. Christ warned…

"If you do not remain in me, you are like a branch that is thrown away and withers; such branches are picked up, thrown into the fire and burned" (John 15:6 NIV).

Are believers eternally secure without any conditions attached to their salvation or are they only eternally secure as they faithfully keep biblical conditions? This is a worthy discussion point. HOWEVER, from the soul-winner's perspective, it doesn't matter which of the above scriptural viewpoints is right, and here is why…

All evangelicals agree on this one truth stated below because it is so clearly backed up by Scripture…

If people are born again and are saved, their life will bear evidence of that!

"He who endures to the end will be saved" (Matthew 10:22).

"If anyone does not abide in Me, he is cast out" (John 15:6).

"Consider the goodness and severity of God... toward you, goodness, if you continue in His goodness. Otherwise you also will be cut off" (Romans 11:22).

"...you are saved, if you hold fast that word which I preached to you-unless you believed in vain" (1 Corinthians 15:2).

"He who says, "I know Him," and does not keep His commandments, is a liar, and the truth is not in him" (1 John 2:4).

"Whoever does not practice righteousness is not of God" (1 John 3:10).

"Whoever transgresses and does not abide in the doctrine of Christ does not have God" (2 John 9).

"He who overcomes shall be clothed in white garments, and I will not blot out his name from The Book of Life" (Revelation 3:5).

From these scriptures, we can only assume that the above dentist was not saved. Whether he was ever saved or not I will leave up to the Ph.D. theologians to debate for now. As soul-winners, however, we must treat those who do not give evidence of salvation as though they are yet unsaved.

We show them what the Word says about how true believers must live. We challenge them to take stock of where they are spiritually. This is scriptural...

"Examine yourselves as to whether you are in the faith. Prove yourselves. Do you not know yourselves, that Jesus Christ is in you?-- Unless indeed, you are disqualified" (2 Corinthians 13:5)?

That's your job, soul-winner, to help people "examine" their lives, in humble submission to God's Word, by which they will one day be eternally judged.

I would have continued to help that dentist see that his soul was in great jeopardy, but he cut himself off from that opportunity with one sentence, "I don't believe in discussing politics or religion." He preferred to take the chance that he could drink his way into heaven by relying on some one-time experience as a child than to even consider repenting of current sins. We know being saved is much more than this!

Whether you believe in the doctrine of eternal security or not, this should not affect how you approach people in witnessing. If they are saved, there will be ample evidence by their words and their deeds. If they aren't saved, then pierce their hearts by quoting biblical truth...

"For the word of God is living and powerful, and sharper than any two-edged sword" (Hebrews 4:12).

Give them as much of the Bible as they will allow you to offer, then the rest is up to them and God.

One of the great tragedies and disappointments in soul-winning is the backslider. A high percentage of those who will pray some prayer, but never become disciples of Christ or get locked-in to a local church is a real challenge to all Christians.

As a soulwinner, you don't have ultimate control over anyone's eternal destiny. Moreover, God does not expect you to do more than you can.

Hence, the most important thing you can do is to make sure that, up-front, one clearly understands the gospel before you encourage them to embrace it. Once they embrace it, you can systematically, patiently counsel them in the biblically standardized Christian maintenance program.

Make it very clear, as this chapter instructs you, what new believers need to do after they have made their decision for Christ. You can pray for them, keep in touch with them, continue to encourage them to attend church, and be available to them. Beyond that, it is up to them and the Lord. Nevertheless...

Follow up is an indispensable duty of soul-winner!

22

REACHING MORMONS
AND JEHOVAH'S WITNESSES

"But...there will be false teachers among you, who will secretly put forward wrong teachings for your destruction, even turning away from the Lord who gave himself for them; whose destruction will come quickly, and they themselves will be the cause of it" (2 Peter 2:1 BBE).

WINNING MORMONS TO CHRIST

A fond memory from when I was a youth minister in Upland was when Kathy and I went calling on a teenage girl who had visited our church. She was a Mormon, but accepted the Lord into her life. As we discussed her relationship with the Mormon Church, she realized that she could not serve Christ and be a Mormon anymore. She wanted to go tell them, so we all piled in my car and drove to her now previous church.

After finding some "elders" who happened to be in the building, we walked up to one of them and explained the decision that she had made. The elder informed us, "Oh, you just can't leave the church like this. There are some steps you must take." I don't know if they were going to sue her or what, but she had had enough and we unceremoniously closed the conversation and walked out of the building. She joyfully put the Mormon church behind her. Knowing what the Mormon church believed helped me convince her of the need to make a "clean break" from the cult.

Unfortunately, you are probably wasting your time arguing with Mormon missionaries. In over half-a-century, I have never won one to Christ. But a jack-Mormon, that is a Mormon backslider or non-practicing Mormon, dissatisfied Mormons or those beginning to examine their Mormon faith are excellent soul-winning prospects. You might start by saying something to them like this: "What if I can prove to you that Joseph Smith is a false prophet?" or "What if I can prove that the Book of Mormon contradicts the Bible?" Then proceed to show how the Bible proves that Mormonism is incorrect.

Below, Mormon doctrines are listed in bold print followed by the verses which disprove and show their doctrinal error.

- **The Bible is our only source of truth.** II Tim. 3:15-17, Matt. 24:35, John 5:39, 12:48.

- **Why Christians cannot accept the Book of Mormon.** Deut. 4:2, 12:32, Rev. 22:18, 19, Prov. 30:5, 6. God warned us against false prophets. Matt. 24:11, 1 Cor. 14:37.

- **Joseph Smith's testimony contradicts Scripture.** 1 Tim. 4:1, Isa. 8:20. He claimed to receive gospel from an angel. II Cor. 11:14, Gal. 1:8. He claimed to see the Father. 1 John 4:12, 1 Tim. 6:16, Ex. 33:20.

- **Joseph Smith taught polygamy and celestial marriage.** Gen. 2:24, 1 Tim. 3:12, Matt. 19:3-9, Mk. 10:2-8, Matt. 22:23-30, Luke 20:34, 35, 1 Cor. 7:6-9, 25-28.

- **He also taught that there are many gods**. Gen. 1:1, 16, Deut. 6:4, Isa. 43:10, 11, 44:6, 45:18. Joseph Smith taught that the Father has flesh and bones. John 4:24, Luke 24:39.

- **The Mormon Church still has Aaronic and Melchizedekian priesthoods.** Heb. 7:1-3. Notice the requirement for this priesthood. Heb. 7:11, 12. The priesthood has been changed. Heb. 7: 18-25. Jesus has fulfilled the types of the priesthood. Heb. 7:27. We no longer need the old priesthoods: their purpose is fulfilled. Heb. 8:13. We are under a new covenant.

- **Mormons teach that all men will eventually be saved and end up in one of three eternal glories, except for a few "sons of perdition."** Matt. 7:13, 14, Rev. 20:11-15, Luke 13:23, 24.

- **Mormons teach that as long as you live a good life and don't reject the truth, you will still escape perdition, because the resurrection of Christ assures all men of resurrection to life.** Mark 16:16, John 3:36, II Thess. 2:12.

- **Mormons believe that everyone has a chance after death, thus, the purpose of baptism for the dead.** Luke 16:22-31, Ezek. 18:20, Heb. 9:27.

- **Jesus Christ is said to be just one of many sons of God.** John 1:1-3, Isa. 9:6, Micah 5:2, Rev. 22:13, Matt. 1:23, Col. 1:16, 17.

- **Salvation is taught to be the result of good works.** Since most everybody is saved, they mean exaltation, or one's position in future worlds. Eph. 2:8, 9, Rom. 4:3-5, Titus 3:5.

Finally, if they are responding favorably, and will allow you to do so, give them one of the presentations of the gospel as shown in Chapter 20 – "Dea's Detour".

WINNING JEHOVAH'S WITNESSES TO CHRIST

You are probably wasting your breath arguing with a Jehovah's Witness who has knocked at your door. They are literally "brain washed" and instructed on how to deal with people who dare try to prove them wrong. But, if you find a dissatisfied witness or someone studying with them who hasn't yet joined their Kingdom Hall, by any means rescue them if you possibly can.

You might start by asking, "May I show you some verses in the Bible that I am certain the witnesses didn't show you?" You'll see how the Bible disproves every major belief of the Jehovah's Witnesses.

Below, the Jehovah's Witnesses' false doctrines are listed in bold followed by Bible texts that prove that doctrine is untrue.

Jehovah's Witnesses teach the following...

- **Jesus was created and had a beginning**. John 1:1, 14, 8:58, 12:34, Micah 5:2

- **Jesus is not God**. Col. 2:9, John 5:18, 10:30, Matt. 1:21, 23, 1 Tim. 3:16, Jer. 23:5, 6, Phil. 2:5-9, Heb. 1:6, 8, II Cor. 5:19, Isa. 9:6, Gen. 19:24, Hos. 1:7. We know Jesus is God, since Jesus is to be worshipped, proving He must be God. Matt. 4:10, Deut. 6:13, Acts 10:25-26, Rev. 22:9, Matt. 8:2, 15:25, 28:9, John 20:28, 29. Jesus is omnipresent, which proves He is God. Col. 1:26-28, Matt. 18:20.

- **The Holy Spirit is just the power of God in operation, and not God Himself, a person.** The Holy Spirit is referred to as "He". John 15:26, 16:1, 13, 14, Acts 5:3, 4; 13:2, 3. The Holy Spirit has a mind. 1 Cor. 2:10, 11; He speaks. Gal. 4:6, Rev. 2:7, Acts 13:2. He intercedes. Rom. 8:26, 27. He teaches. 1 Cor. 2:13. He is mentioned in Scripture separately from the power of God. Luke 1:35, 1 Thess. 1:5. He comforts. John 14:16, 26. He can be tempted. Acts 5:9. He can be lied to. Acts 5:3. He can be ignored. Eph. 4:30. He can be insulted. Heb. 10:29. Thus, the Holy Spirit is given many attributes that only a person would have!

- **Christ did not rise from the grave in an actual body.** Luke 24:36-39.

- **Death is annihilation, with no further punishment.** 1 Sam. 28:7-20, Matt. 17:3, 22:31,2, John 11:25, 26, Phil. 1:21-24, Luke 16:19-31, 1 Thess. 4:14-17, Rev. 6:9.

- **Hell is eternal unconsciousness.** Mark 9:48, Isa. 66:24. Rev. 14:11 describes hell as torment "forever and ever." The same words in Greek used in 14:11 translated "forever and ever" are used in Rev. 4:10 describing Christ. If Christ is forever, so must be the torment!

- **Jehovah's Witnesses teach that we are saved by good works.** Eph. 2:8, 9, Titus 3:5, Rom. 5:1, Gal. 3:26, Rom. 6:23, 10:13, John 1:12.

If they have listened with a teachable spirit to you sharing some of the above truths, use these verses also to show them that when we receive Jesus, we are receiving Jehovah: Matt. 9:6, John 5:22, 23, 6:47, 12:44, 45, 13:20, 14:6, 23, 1 John 2:23, 4:15.

Finally, if they are responding favorably, and will allow you to do so, give them one of the presentations of the gospel as shown in Chapter 20 – "Dea's Detour".

Approximately 6.6 million Mormons and 1.2 million Jehovah's Witnesses live in The United States. Many other "Christian" cults exist, but these two are the largest in our nation.

I have carried a burden especially for Mormons for many years. When I drive by their wards, I often pray for God to bring the truth to the people who meet there. God promises,

"And it shall come to pass in the last days, says God, that I will pour out of My Spirit on all flesh" (Acts 2:17).

It is my sincere hope that in the final move of God on our planet "all flesh" will include many people who, like I was, are deceived by false prophets.

I dream of one day preaching the gospel in Mormon churches and Temples!

Photocopy (You have my permission) the above and tape them inside the back of your main Bible for ready reference when the opportunity arises.

Remember, by having these verses in my Bible I was ready to lead that Mormon, Grant Hollist, to Christ.

"Always be prepared to give an answer to everyone who asks you to give the reason for the hope that you have" (1 Peter 3:15 NIV).

Pray for Mormons and Jehovah's Witnesses!

23

SOWING AND REAPING

"Those who sow with tears shall reap with songs of joy! Those who go out weeping, carrying the seed to sow, will return with songs of joy, carrying his sheaves with him"
(Psalms 126:5, 6 NIV).

This book is not an exhaustive study of evangelism. We didn't have time to discuss how you would deal with a Muslim, Buddhist, or an atheist, for instance. We didn't have space to answer all the questions that sinner's frequently ask. You will likely be confronted with a question or contradictory statement that you have no idea how to answer. I have experienced the same countless times.

If you want to arm yourself for the battle to win men's souls, there are many other books written by teachers and evangelists that can help. I have already mentioned several in earlier chapters. You might want to google, search amazon.com or go to your local Christian bookstore for further helps. There are excellent authors to choose from: Norman Geisler, Chris Overstreet, Lee Strobel, Che Ahn, Paul E. Little, Gregory Koukl are but a few among many. Find books by searching under "evangelism, soul-winning, soul winning, apologetics, or witnessing."

The people easiest to win to Christ will be those who already believe the basics of Christianity: the Bible, Jesus, heaven, hell, etc. Since 65% of Americans consider themselves Christian (at least when asked about their religious affiliation), most people you witness to will not respond to your questions with, 'I don't believe in God, Jesus, the Bible, etc." They will already agree with much of what you say.

This book has given you ample information, enabling you to witness effectively to most people. If the Lord has birthed in your heart a greater desire than ever to win the lost, I urge you to continue to study, memorize Scriptures and familiarize yourself with prepared answers to more difficult questions that unbelievers or those of other faiths commonly ask.

Also, this book is primarily written to train and inspire reapers. Reapers are those who consider witnessing as but a means to an end: to personally lead a sinner to Christ. Sowers are just as important though. It has been theorized that it takes seven distinct and different exposures to the gospel before the average sinner comes to Christ. If this is the case, then you can see how other Christians and their ministries help sow to prepare hearts for a time of reaping.

Paul wrote,

"I become all things to all people, that I may save some of them by whatever means are possible" (1 Cor. 9:22 GNT).

"Whatever means" is all-inclusive. Could you or your church use any of these methods below to either overtly or subtly sow the truth of the gospel?

Sowing The Gospel Truth

Theater, live plays, Christian themed movies, Sunday church services in the park, home Bible studies, internet teachings, YouTube videos, Facebook posts, Twitter messages, outdoor drive-in services, church banquets, socials, church baseball leagues, talent shows, booths in fairs, park outreaches with music or drama, tables set up in public with literature like Jehovah's Witnesses do, booths set up to interpret dreams or pray with people, bumper stickers or t-shirts with a gospel message, letter writing, artwork, books, tracts, and any or all written materials, and on and on.

Can you see something on that list you can do? Could you add your own creative idea to that list, one that fits your natural talents and personality? If you for any reason don't feel ready to be a reaper, what can you do now to start sowing seeds of the gospel? Jesus likes sowers: "A sower went out to sow his seed" (Luke 8:5).

Something else, you sower you, which you might consider when you have certain outreaches. On occasions, a brief presentation of the gospel by a reaper, who gives a call for people to commit their lives to Christ, could close out the event. This is providing, of course, that it wouldn't be ridiculously out of place, like at a ball-game! You do your thing and then let someone who has the gift and a proven anointing to pull in the net for the lost.

In frontier days of early America, a preacher would preach the gospel and when he was done, the pulpit would be turned over to someone they called "an exhorter." The exhorter, the reaper, would then invite people to come to the altar. This idea was taken from the list of ministries in Romans 12:8 which included "He who exhorts." Your pastor can help you decide when this might be appropriate or even do the reaping for you…or hire me!

A case in point of how to turn a sowing opportunity into a reaping opportunity would be the "Horrorthon" that our youth group did when I was Minister of Youth in Upland, CA. Youth came for fun, food, and games, but then at the end of the celebrations, I stood up and preached a short gospel message. I then gave an altar call for those who wanted to come to Christ to step forward and many did. But then, I am a reaper.

Above: In Darby, MT, a crew of youth in town for a summer work project all visited a service. Many, as shown, made a decision for Christ when I operated in the gift of a "reaper."

To be clear, sowing in itself is a God-ordained method of evangelism, with or without adding any attempts at reaping. If sowing is within your comfort zone at the present, just keep on doing it without condemnation, with joy and with faith because of this precious promise:

"Therefore, my beloved brethren, be steadfast, immovable, always abounding in the work of the Lord, knowing that your labor is not in vain in the Lord" (Corinthians 15:58).

Passing Out Tracts

My wife's favorite TV preacher, Joyce Meyer, says, "Going door to door and handing out tracts is not my gift. I'll just stand back there quietly." That is from a woman who preaches regularly before thousands! Everybody has their talents from the Lord. If you think you might be able to go door to door, try it. If you can't hand out tracts to strangers, you can at least "hide" them places, leave them behind with a tip, send them when paying bills, etc.

While preaching decades ago, I mentioned from the pulpit the minimal effects I had from passing out tracts. After the service, a woman approached me to tell me a story. She said that she was in a K-Mart looking at shirts and picked up one that had a tract inside the pocket. She pulled it out, read it, and came to Christ as a result! That was before I had written my own tract and passed them out around the nation as I travelled. I certainly believe in tracts now!

My son Nathan was about to graduate from high school when he developed a burden for souls. All his best friends were unsaved, one was a Mormon. He had been wondering if God wanted him to enter the ministry and become a soul-winner. One day, while walking around a cinema foyer before watching a movie, he looked up at the ceiling and said,

"Lord, do you want me to become a soul-winner?"

Within seconds, a boy about 12 years old walked over to him and asked him, "Do you know Jesus?" He then handed my son a tract. Taking this as a sign from the Lord, Nathan decided to go to Bible College that next semester and, yes, he has since won souls! Sadly, my son said that boy who gave him a tract, was only the second person in his life who ever witnessed to him! May God change the American Church's soul-winning habits!

Nathan with youth in Asia

Nathan has since been to the mission field several times with YWAM and to Thailand to help a missionary there for five months. He has studied Japanese and Chinese. He even won a fellow Chinese college student to Christ! Nathan carries a burden for Asia and is currently waiting on God for his next assignment.

Don't tell me handing out tracts is a waste of time!

I remind you of the story when I was working out at a gym and gave a young man my tract. He called me that same evening to tell me how excited he and his father were about what they had read. A few days later, I was in their living room, kneeling at the coffee table leading them both to Christ.

As a reaper, as an evangelist, as a soul-winner, I have seen little visible fruit through the years from passing out tracts. My tract, on the other hand, when used as a door-opener to give further witness and share the gospel has helped me lead I don't know how many to Christ. Hand a tract to someone and watch where it can lead!

Even if after reading this whole book you are not convinced that you can be a soul-winner, you can nevertheless let tracts preach the gospel for you!

Turn to my sample tract now at the back of this book. Take a sneak-preview of it. You'll see that I included two copies of the tract so that you could cut one out to make copies for yourself or your church and still leave one copy in the book permanently. I'll explain later how to do this.

Still doubting your ability to witness for Christ?

It is possible that after everything I have written and shared, you still lack confidence to be a bold witness for Christ. I want to close this chapter by leaving you with this truth. Paul was struggling with some very difficult things, so he asked the Lord about it. The Lord told him,

""My grace is sufficient for you, for My strength is made perfect in weakness" (2 Corinthians 12:9).

Just as sinners are saved by grace, so also your ability to evangelize sinners is a work of grace! Pray for God's grace to strengthen you in those areas of your personality that make it difficult for you to witness.

"But we have this wealth in vessels of earth, so that it may be seen that the power comes not from us but from God" (2 Corinthians 4:7 BBE). Don't lean on the energy of your flesh, learn to by faith access the power to witness that comes only from God!

"You shall receive power after the Holy Spirit has come upon you and you shall be witnesses to me" (Acts 1:8).

Seek to be a person always filled with the Holy Spirit, and you are guaranteed to be a "witness" for Him.

Above: From left to right: Kathy, me, my daughter, Carissa and her
husband, Andy, at their 2007 wedding.

My whole family at Disneyland, 2017. From left to right: Andy Hawksworth: my son-in-law, Kathy: my wife, Luke: my grandson, Nathan: my son, Caden: my grandson, Carissa: my daughter, and me.

24

UNFINISHED BUSINESS

"Knowing therefore, the terror of the Lord, we persuade
men...For the love of Christ constrains us...God...has
committed to us the word...Therefore we are ambassadors for
Christ, as though God were pleading through us: we implore
you on Christ's behalf, be reconciled to God"
(2 Corinthians 5:11, 14, 20).

As I wrote this book, I thought the previous chapter was my last. However, I was finishing up the final touches of the book for formatting and publishing, then something happened this morning. I realized the Lord had given me one more experience to share with you, which I'll do shortly.

Aimee Semple McPherson, a great soul-winner, built the biggest church of her time. Do you think she knew her business? She said,

"The one big business of the church is evangelism."

Evangelism is BIG, in importance, business indeed! Yet, evangelism is also like a small family-owned business. Families have their times of fellowship, encouraging one another, conversation around the dinner table, and enjoying their life together. Yet, daily, each family member must head out to fulfill their unique duties to keep their business open and make it successful. The church is a family-owned business. We "go home" to church where we join together to sing, worship, pray, study the Bible, encourage and uplift one another. Then, we go to work to do our part in our one big family business, world-evangelism. So...

MIND YOUR OWN BUSINESS!

As I write this chapter, I am in Phoenix, Arizona. I went for an early morning prayer walk. After getting coffee at the Circle-K near my motel, a man approached me and asked if I had a quarter. I figured that he was an alcoholic wanting a drink. His face was deeply tanned and wizened from the Arizona desert sun, living on the street, and many years of daily drinking. He was about the same age and looked very much like my nephew, Shane, whom I told you about earlier. God gave me compassion for this man, so I told him "I don't give money to people I don't know."

However, I offered to buy him food if he was hungry. No, he didn't want any food. Drunks don't eat much. Then I said, "I am an evangelist. I can help you spiritually if you want." I began to share how God had delivered my dad and my brother from alcoholism and that God could deliver him too. I started quoting John 8:36, "...if the Son makes you free, you shall be free indeed." He said, "thank you" and turned to walk away.

I continued my prayer walk, taking sips of my coffee. I asked God for more power, more wisdom, and to help me win souls. The man's face was still emblazoned on my mind. He looked so much like my nephew, who likely was weeping in hell at that very moment. Then, it came to me, I had approached the man offering him deliverance from alcohol, but he didn't want that! However, I had not brought up the most important deliverance of all, deliverance from eternal hell. Turning around, I walked back toward the Circle-K hoping I would run into him again. I found him sitting at a bus stop in front of the store.

I did something that I don't think I had ever done before, but I was desperate! "For if we are beside ourselves, it is for God" (2 Corinthians 5:13). I said to him, "Look, what you do with your money is none of my business. But if you will let me talk with you about the Lord for a while, I'll give you some money." He said, "No, thanks." His emergency over, a pint of hard liquor hidden in a brown bag (so the police wouldn't think he was being publicly-intoxicated), was already in his hand. Even though he wasn't interested, I just could not let it end there. I began to preach to him anyway, without his permission.

"The love of Christ compels us" (2 Corinthians 5:14).

After explaining the gospel, I asked him if he would like to accept Christ into his heart. He said he did.

I began leading him to follow me in a sinner's prayer. When I suggested that he admit to Christ, "I'm an alcoholic" he instead said "I'm a drunk."

When I, as usual, asked him to say, "I admit I'm a sinner," he stopped praying. Then, he bluntly said, "That's enough!" I knew he wasn't ready to repent, so I left it there. I gave him my tract and asked him if he would read it. He said he would. It reminds me of Paul's experience with Felix:

"Now as he reasoned about righteousness, self-control, and the judgment to come, Felix was afraid and answered, 'Go away for now'" (Acts 24:25).

Paul preached grace, but he also preached "righteousness, self-control, and the judgment to come."

Don't try to make it easy on sinners. You might, but the devil sure won't! "Go away for now" is what that drunk told me. He showed some interest, but that "self-control" aspect of the gospel was just something, like Felix, that he wasn't ready for. And many that you try to reach out to will tell you the same.

Until a sinner dies, he still has a chance. Maybe the next person doing the work of an evangelist can convince that Christ-rejecting man to repent at last, before it's everlastingly too late. Prepare yourself for rejections. Don't take it personally! If the greatest apostle, Paul, couldn't convince Felix, and a seasoned evangelist, Dea, couldn't convince a drunk, please understand that much of your ministry will also remain unfinished business.

For the next two days, each time I went by the Circle-K, I saw him sitting at that bus stop. Early in the morning, as I was leaving Phoenix to return home, he was still sitting, half-asleep on that bench. I walked over to him and greeted him, shook his hand and asked him if he had read my tract. He said he had, and then pulled it part way out of his pocket and said, "I still have it." It was already soiled from two days of dirt, sun and sweat. But he had kept it! That gave me hope.

I asked, and he permitted me to take his picture. I told him I would be praying for him, then left. I'm quite sure I'll never see him again. I am reminded of Jesus' burden for the residents of Jerusalem when He said…

"Oh Jerusalem, Jerusalem…How often I wanted to gather your children together, as a hen gathers her chicks under her wings, but you were not willing" (Matthew 23:37).

A lost man from Phoenix, like those in Jerusalem, was "not willing." His portrait is on the last page of this chapter. His face epitomizes and graphically represents all that I have sought to communicate to you, my reader. I felt the Lord gave it to me for this book as a fitting final tribute to personal evangelism.

I added the pictures of many people throughout this book. I wanted you to "see" that soul-winning is all about real people, hurting people, dying people, people whose smiling faces might instead be soon frowning throughout eternity in hell. That is, unless we do our part to help add the joy of salvation to their lives.

Consider this. Even today, someone may walk up to you and request something of you, money, directions, help. Ask yourself, "Is this a God-appointed witnessing opportunity?" Be watchful for such times! Or you may be walking away from someone, as I did, and feel the "love of Christ" compelling you to return once again, this time with greater boldness, to speak to them about their soul.

Make their eternal destiny your personal business!
It is!

Evangelist is the title of this book. Evangelist is also my title full-time. It is what my life-long journey was all about.

Now, it is my hope that you understand and believe that Evangelist is your title as well, at least part-time.

God grant that soul-winning adventures, as in my journey, will also be important milestones in your own journey.

Evangelism is what an evangelist does. It is his or her business. As a member of the body of Christ, it is your business also.

When you turn the page you'll see a picture that is typical of too many American tragedies. We can and MUST change that!

In closing, may I, at risk of being too redundant, remind you one more time that you are called to…

"Do the work of an evangelist" (2 Timothy 4:5).

UNFINISHED BUSINESS: He called himself "a drunk" but he could be a child of the King. Let's do our best to help people like him escape from a wasted life and an eternity in hell!

EPILOGUE

Jack Hayford helped me write this book by teaching me how to "do the work of an evangelist" as a 17-year old new convert. I have one more story about Jack that I must share. It's a final way to say, "Thank you, Brother Hayford for so dramatically influencing my life." His words motivated me. I think they will do the same for you. This last story is also a fitting epilogue for

Evangelist My Life Story: My Life Journey.

On that unforgettable day when Jack stood before our college classroom seeking to motivate us to be the Lord's witnesses, he quoted Ezekiel 3:18,

"When I say to the wicked, 'You shall surely die,' and you give him no warning, nor speak to warn the wicked from his wicked way, to save his life, that same wicked man shall die in his iniquity; but his blood I will require at your hand."

Reaching both his hands towards us, with palms up, as we stood in rapt attention, he then warned,

"At the judgment many of us will have our hands literally dripping with blood."

You are not an Ezekiel. You are not responsible for every wicked person you may run across. However, you likely will one day soon meet someone that the Lord put in your path. In your spirit, you will know that God wants you to share the gospel with them, then and there. At that moment you literally, like Aaron interceding for dying Israelites, will be standing…

"…between the dead and the living" (Numbers 16:48).

You will be accountable, not for what they do about your witness, but what you do about it! May God give us all grace that we might on that judgment day, say with Paul the Apostle,

"Therefore I testify to you this day that I am innocent of the blood of all men" (Acts 20:26).

On the next 4 pages are two copies of my "Where and When" tract. Make a million copies if you want! There are two copies so that you can leave one in the book permanently.

Cut out the other one using a thin, long piece of thin metal or plastic behind the page (to keep you from cutting through other pages).

With a razor blade, cut it as closely as you can to the bookbinding. Then, you are welcome to print up as many copies as you want from your printer.

Use my tract as the master and copy both sides of it. Set the original and the copy properly aligned on your copier so that you have two tracts per 8 1/2" X 11 piece of paper.

Make sure you have the front one side, then the back on the opposite side. Center it so that all you will need to do is to cut the copied page in half. You can trim it around the edges if you want to make it smaller.

Then be sure to add your personal contact information or your church's information on the back blank space of the tract.

If you prefer a more professional looking copy, you can order the tract for...

$6.00 per 100 in black and white or

$10.00 per 100 in color (plus shipping)

Order them from our professional printer here in California....

His Print Media Ministries

www.tracts4u.com

PH: 805-452-5150.

Where and When...were you born? Everybody knows the answer to that question. But here is a harder one: where and when were you born again? Knowing that answer is crucial because Jesus said there is only one way to get into heaven, "Unless a man is born again, he shall not see the kingdom of God" (John 3:3). If you know where and when you were born, but aren't 100% sure you were ever born again, the Bible shows you how. Being born again is like the birth of a baby: one day, in a dark womb, the next day, living in the light! "He has called you out of darkness and into His marvelous light" (Romans 3:23).

make in your life. "If anyone is in Christ, he is a new (born) creation. Old things are passed away. All things are new" (2 Cor. 5:17). "Old things" (like sins) must be put behind you to concentrate on the "new!"

The first thing you need to do is to be BAPTIZED IN WATER by immersion: "Whoever believes (the gospel) and is baptized will be saved" (Mark 16:15, 16). Find a pastor to baptize you and a good church full of fellow believers to join. These are primary ways we follow Christ! Repent, come to Jesus, follow Him, be born again and,

ACT on your decision... Go to church this Sunday! Contact the church or person below for more info...

God is urging you to escape what Christ called "outer darkness" or Hell. "Whoever was not written in the Book of Life was cast into the lake of fire" (Revelation 20:15). A newborn is given a birth-certificate. If you are born again, your name is written in the Book of Life, from which all will be judged. Either hell or heaven is everyone's destiny. Becoming a born-again Christian is the ONLY WAY to avoid Hell and experience eternal light and eternal life. So, is your name written in the Book of Life? If you are in doubt, let the Savior show you what to do about it.

HOW is one BORN AGAIN?

REPENT... Jesus said, "Unless you repent you will... perish" (Luke 13:3). Repent means to turn away from your sins and dedicate yourself to bringing your life in line with Christ's teachings as recorded in the Bible. "The word that I have spoken...will judge him in the last day" (John 12:48). God's Word says you're a sinner, "All have sinned and fall short of the glory (presence) of God" (Romans 3:23). You can't earn the privilege of living in His eternal presence. "He saved us, not because we did the right things, but...by a new birth" (Titus 3:5). Do you think you're good enough in God's

eyes? Think again! "There is no one who does good, no, not one" (Romans 3:12). Do you think that you have a good heart? Think again! "The heart is deceitful above all things and desperately wicked" (Jer. 17:9). God sees a lifetime of anger, pride, hatred, jealousy or lust; and all these are "desperately wicked" to God! Because of these sins you'll one day face a payday. "The wages of sin is (eternal) death" (Romans 6:23). All the good deeds you may have done in the past can never compensate, in God's eyes, for your past sins. But it's not too late for you! You have a Savior, Jesus!

Come to Jesus... He invites you personally, "Come to me" (Matt. 11:28). Once you come to Jesus and "repent and believe the gospel" (Mark 1:15), He will receive you and forgive you of all sins. "If we confess our sins, He is faithful to forgive us and to cleanse us from all unrighteousness" (1 John 1:9). Confess all sins and call on Him, "Everyone who calls on the name of the Lord will be saved" (Romans 10:13). Humbly pray NOW, "God be merciful to me a sinner" (Luke 18:13).

Follow Jesus... He invites you to "follow me" (John 8:12). When you're born again, you show your faith and sincerity to follow Christ by the changes you now make in your life. "If anyone is in Christ, he is a new (born) creation. Old things are passed away. All things are new" (2 Cor. 5:17). "Old things" (like sins) must be put behind you to concentrate on the "new!"

The first thing you need to do is to be BAPTIZED IN WATER by immersion: "Whoever believes (the gospel) and is baptized will be saved" (Mark 16:15, 16). Find a pastor to baptize you and a good church full of fellow believers to join. These are primary ways we follow Christ! Repent, come to Jesus, follow Him, be born again and,

ACT on your decision... Go to church this Sunday! Contact the church or person below for more info...

Where and When...were you born? Everybody knows the answer to that question. But here is a harder one: where and when were you born again? Knowing that answer is crucial because Jesus said there is only one way to get into heaven, "Unless a man is born again, he shall not see the kingdom of God" (John 3:3). If you know where and when you were born, but aren't 100% sure you were ever born again, the Bible shows you how. Being born again is like the birth of a baby: one day, in a dark womb, the next day, living in the light! "He has called you out of darkness and into His marvelous light" (Romans 3:23).

God is urging you to escape what Christ called "outer darkness" or Hell. "Whoever was not written in the Book of Life was cast into the lake of fire" (Revelation 20:15). A newborn is given a birth-certificate. If you are born again, your name is written in the Book of Life, from which all will be judged. Either hell or heaven is everyone's destiny. Becoming a born-again Christian is the ONLY WAY to avoid Hell and experience eternal light and eternal life. So, is your name written in the Book of Life? If you are in doubt, let the Savior show you what to do about it.

HOW is one BORN AGAIN?

REPENT... Jesus said, "Unless you repent you will... perish" (Luke 13:3). Repent means to turn away from your sins and dedicate yourself to bringing your life in line with Christ's teachings as recorded in the Bible. "The word that I have spoken...will judge him in the last day" (John 12:48). God's Word says you're a sinner, "All have sinned and fall short of the glory (presence) of God" (Romans 3:23). You can't earn the privilege of living in His eternal presence. "He saved us, not because we did the right things, but...by a new birth" (Titus 3:5). Do you think you're good enough in God's

eyes? Think again! "There is no one who does good, no, not one" (Romans 3:12). Do you think that you have a good heart? Think again! "The heart is deceitful above all things and desperately wicked" (Jer. 17:9). God sees a lifetime of anger, pride, hatred, jealousy or lust; and all these are "desperately wicked" to God! Because of these sins you'll one day face a payday. "The wages of sin is (eternal) death" (Romans 6:23). All the good deeds you may have done in the past can never compensate, in God's eyes, for your past sins. But it's not too late for you! You have a Savior, Jesus!

Come to Jesus... He invites you personally, "Come to me" (Matt. 11:28). Once you come to Jesus and "repent and believe the gospel" (Mark 1:15), He will receive you and forgive you of all sins. "If we confess our sins, He is faithful to forgive us and to cleanse us from all unrighteousness" (1 John 1:9). Confess all sins and call on Him, "Everyone who calls on the name of the Lord will be saved" (Romans 10:13). Humbly pray NOW, "God be merciful to me a sinner" (Luke 18:13).

Follow Jesus... He invites you to "follow me" (John 8:12). When you're born again, you show your faith and sincerity to follow Christ by the changes you now

"Go into all the world and preach the gospel to every creature. He who believes and is baptized will be saved; but he who does not believe will be condemned... And they went out and preached everywhere, the Lord working with them and confirming the word."

(Mark 16:15, 16, 20)

Evangelist Dea Warford

E-mail: warford7@hotmail.com

To receive Dea's daily E-mail teachings in your inbox, free of charge, sign up today by going to our website:

www.deawarford.com

You may also order more copies of this book in paperback k, hardback, or E-book at our website, or at amazon.com.